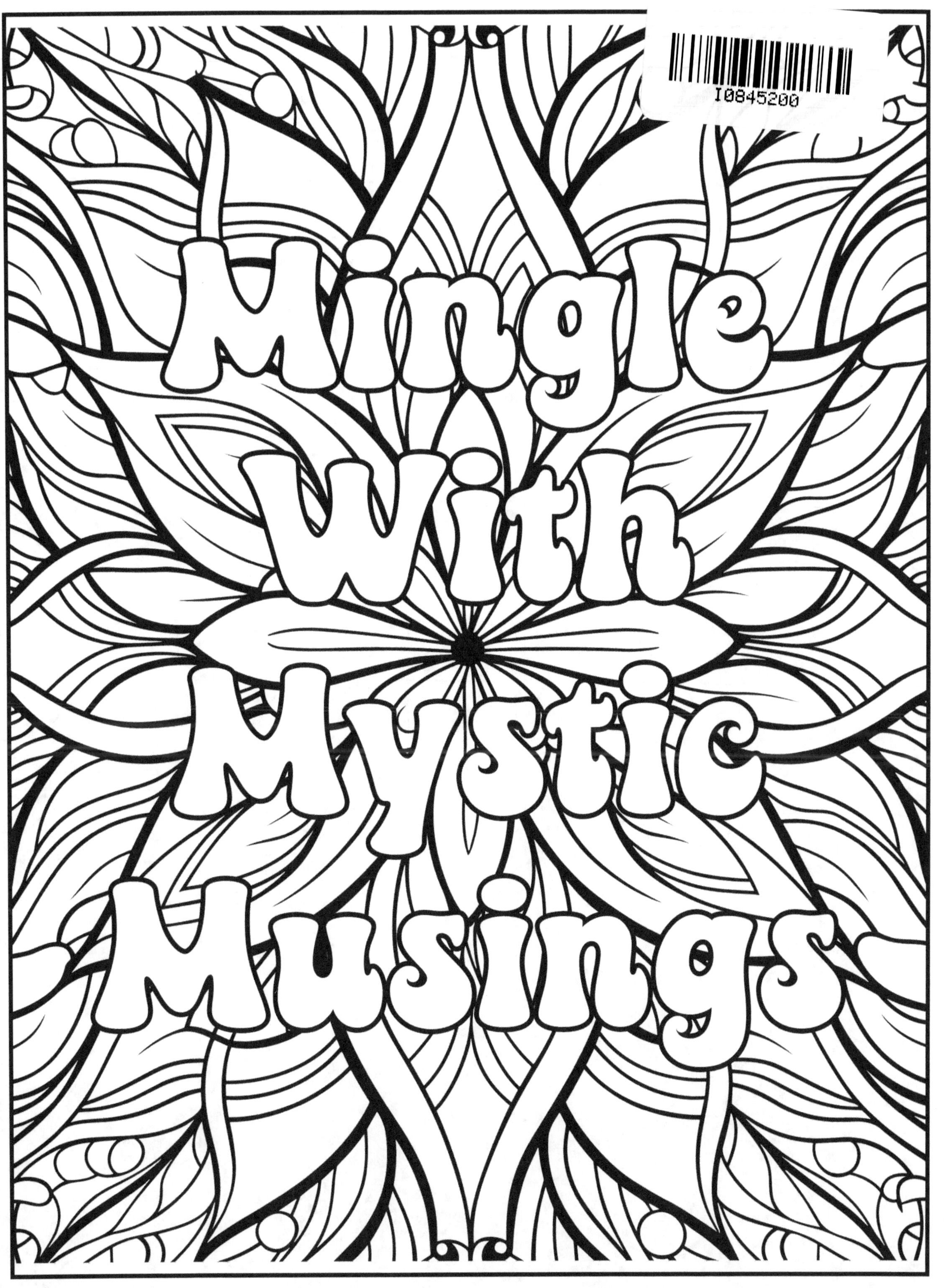

Mingle With Mystic Musings

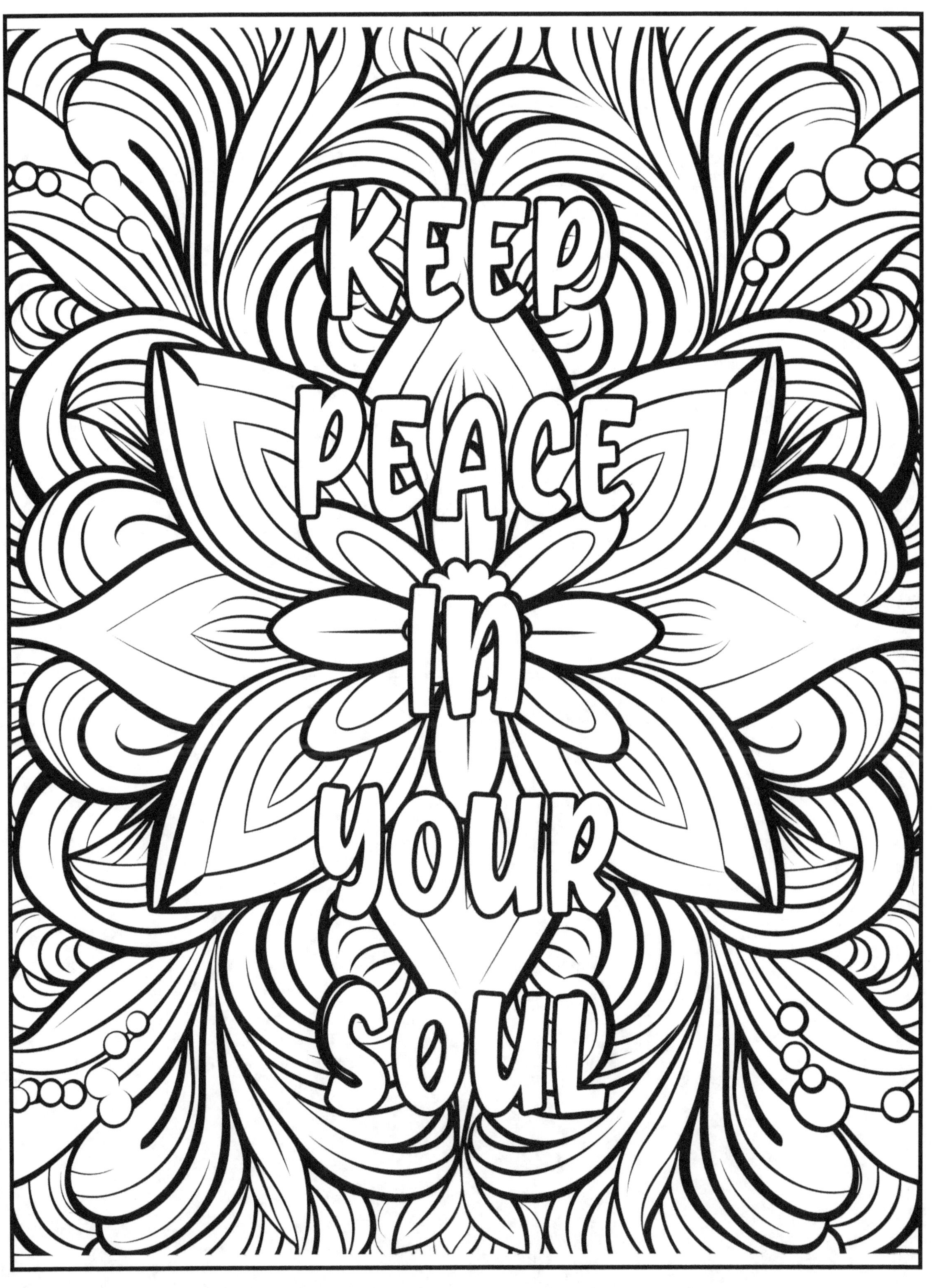

KEEP
PEACE
IN
YOUR
SOUL

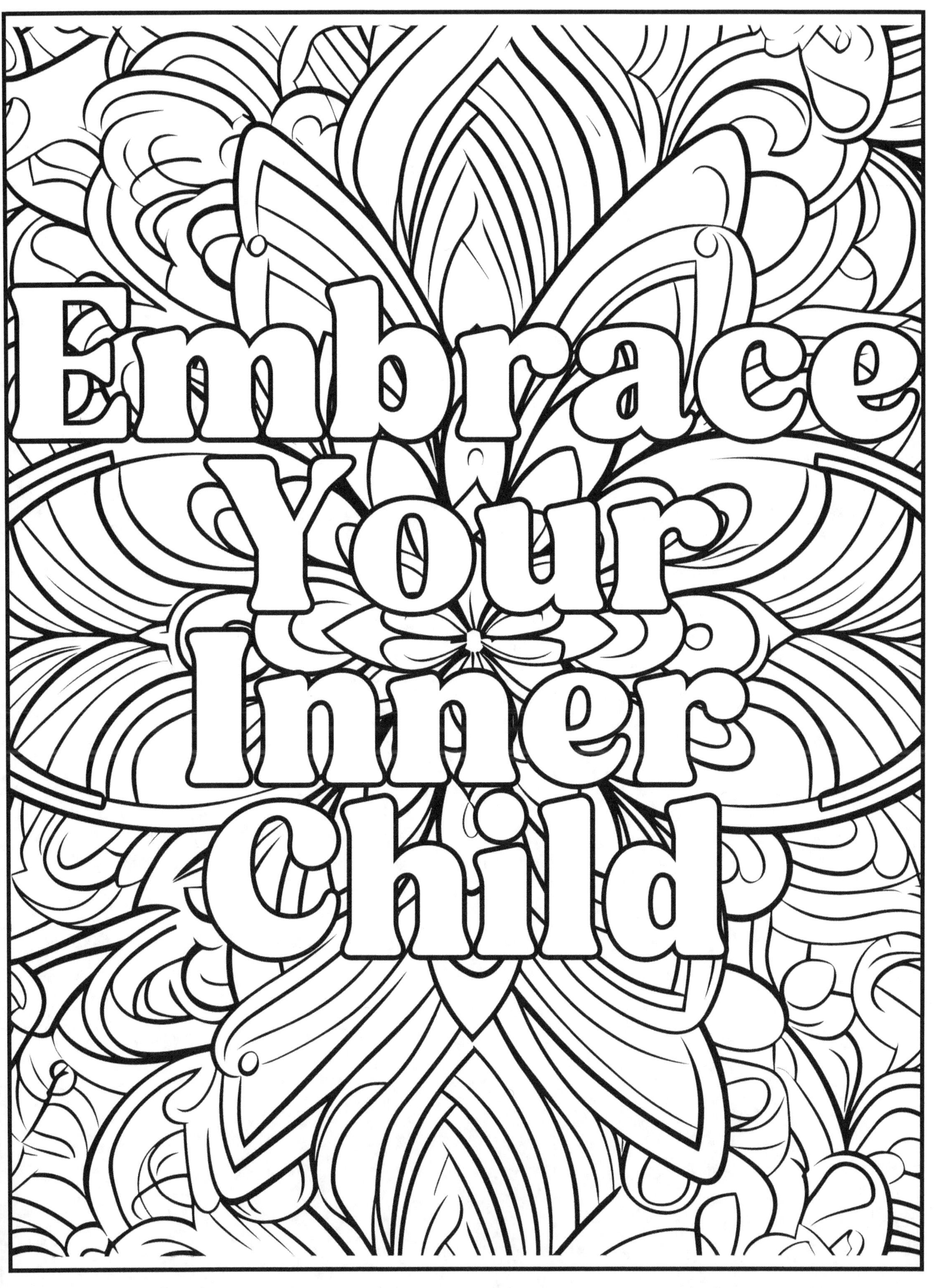

Embrace
Your
Inner
Child

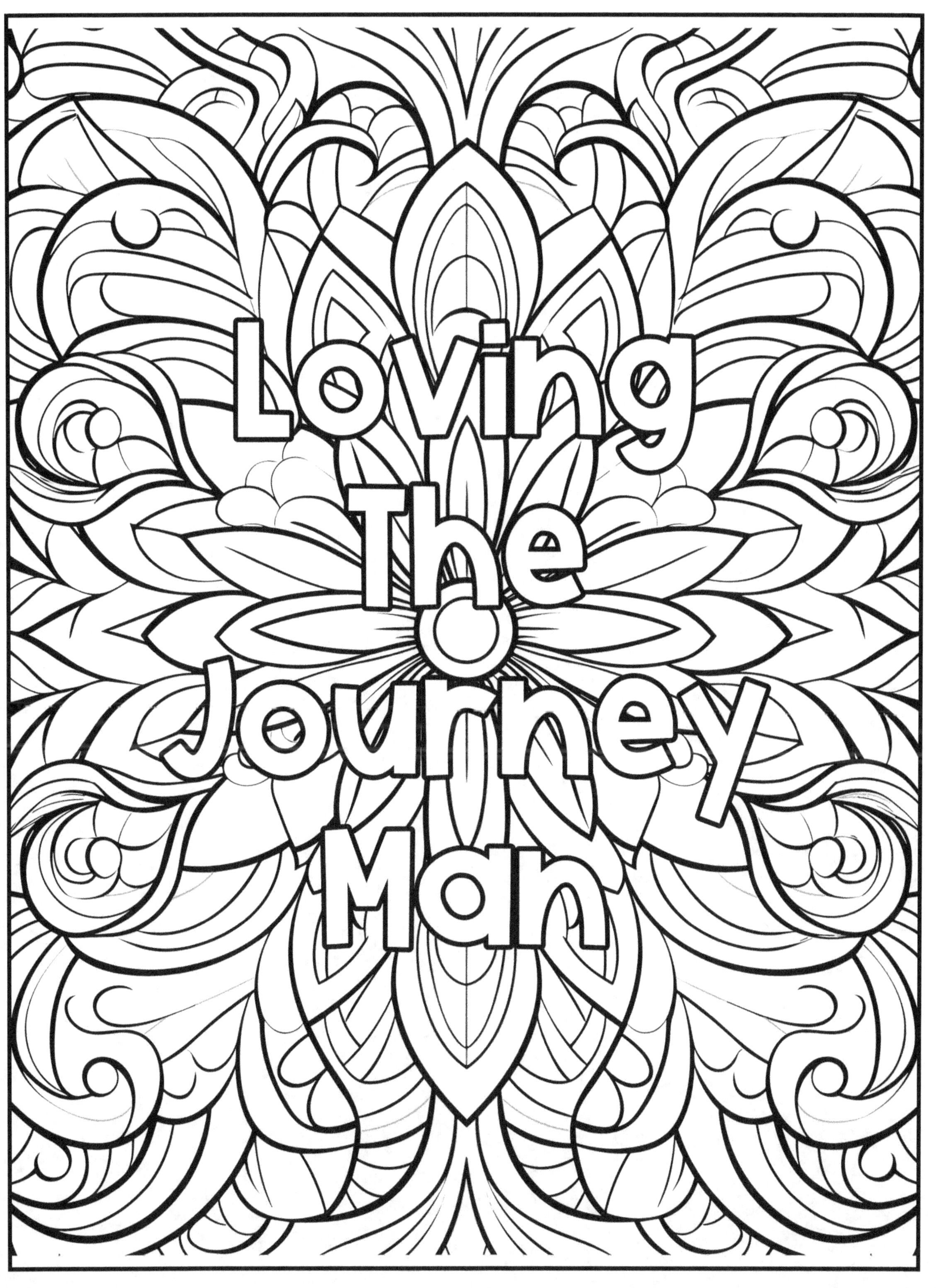

Loving
The
Journey
Man

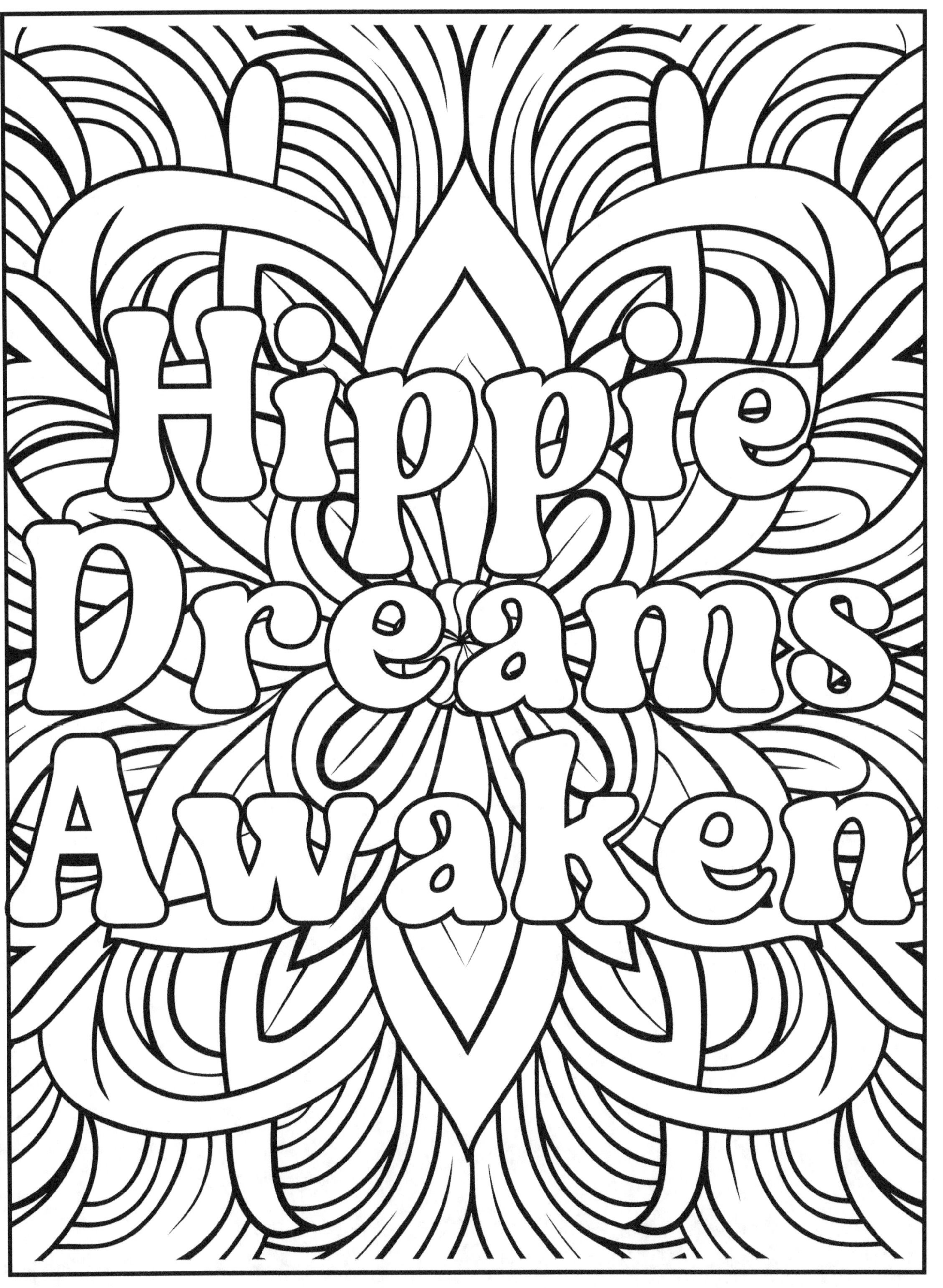

Hippie
Dreams
Awaken

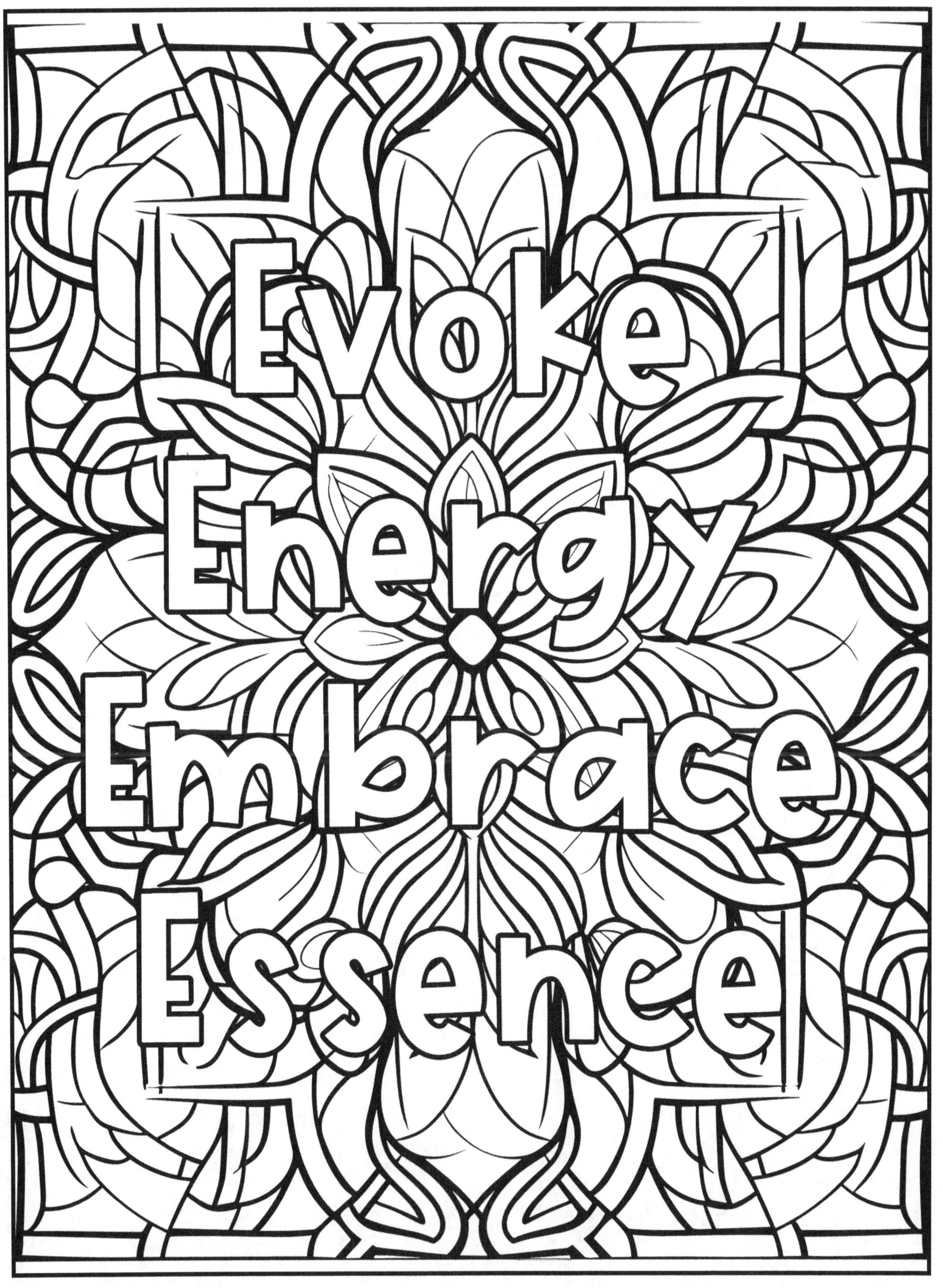

Evoke
Energy
Embrace
Essence

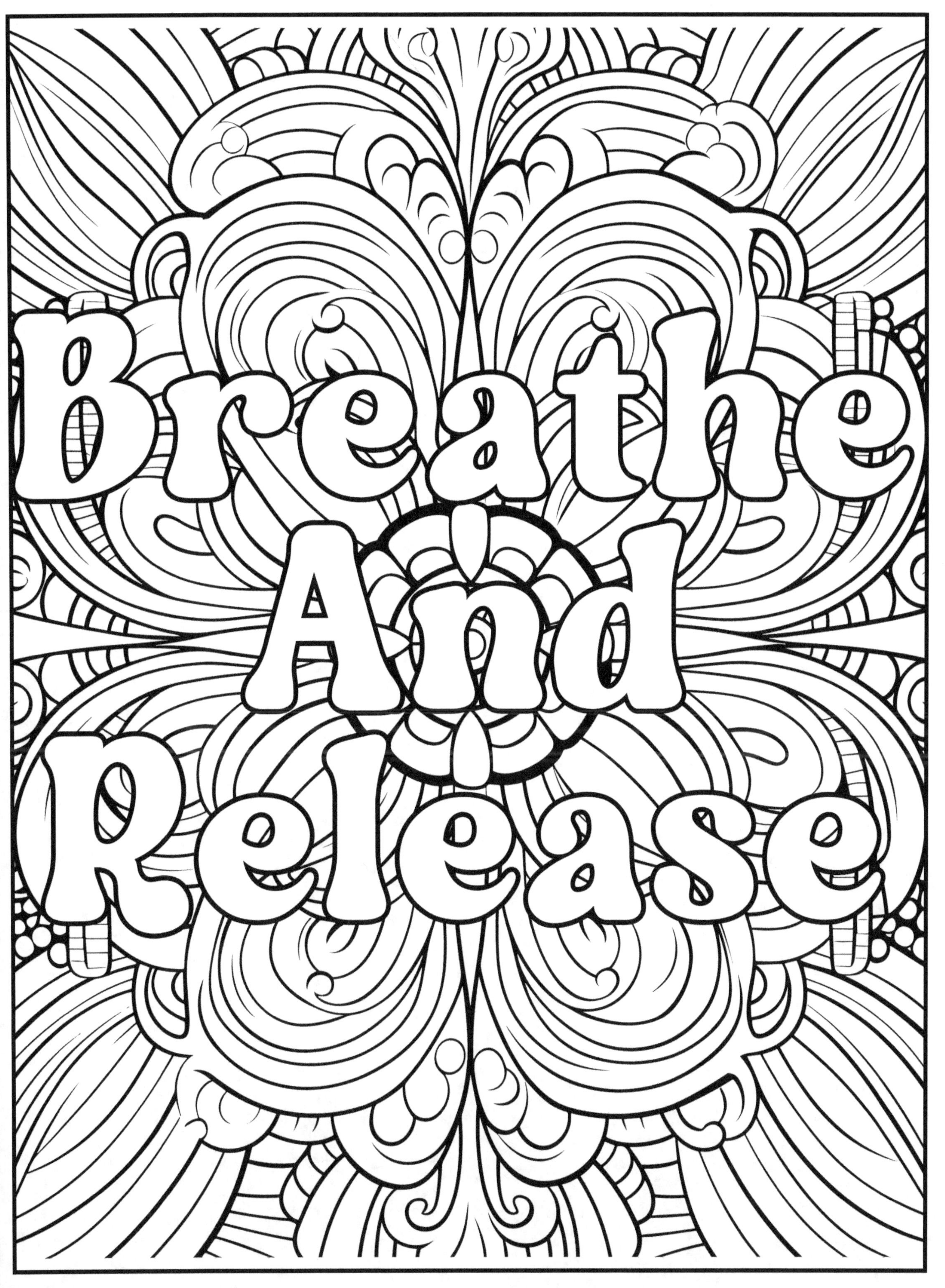

Breathe
And
Release

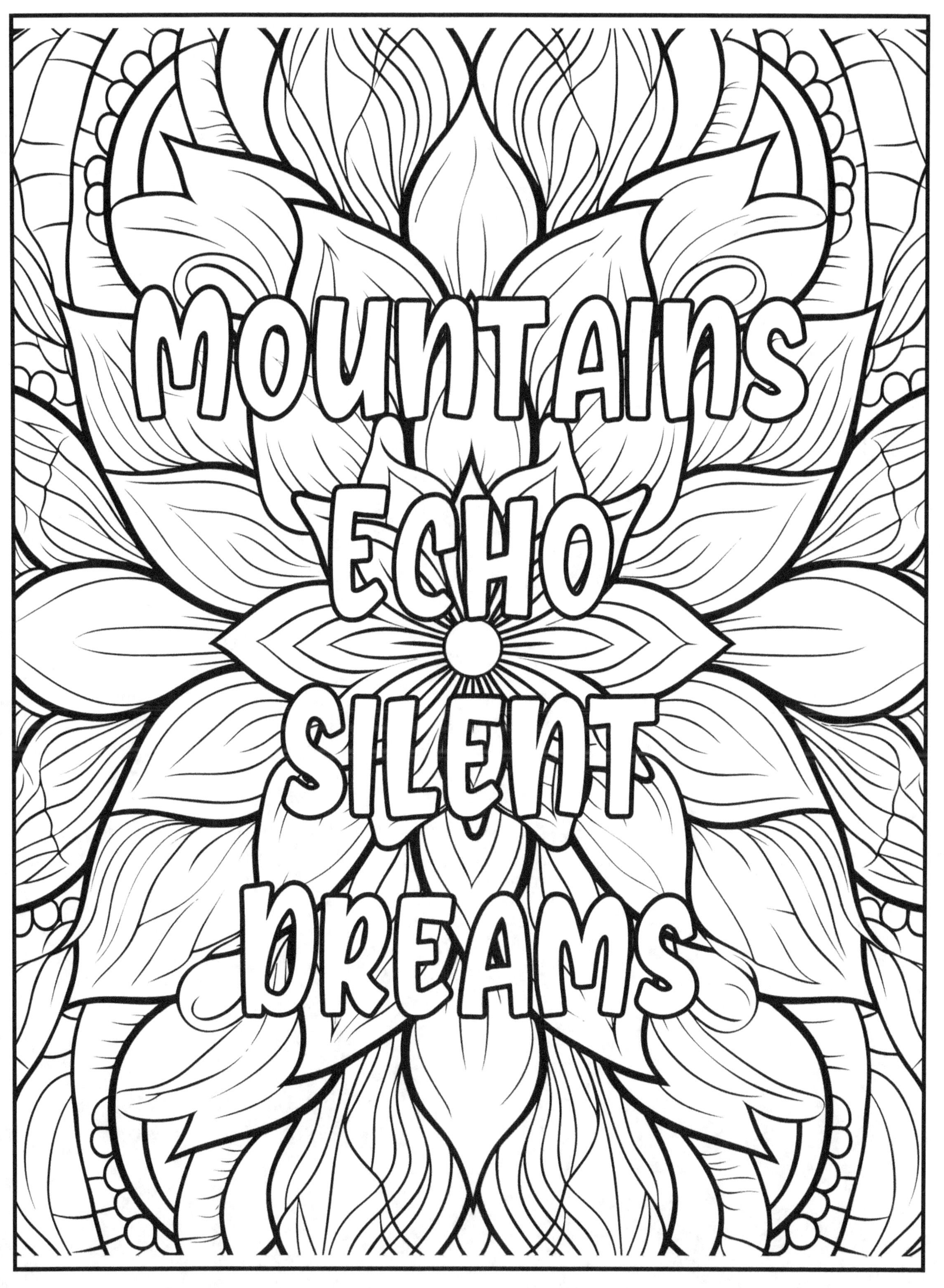

MOUNTAINS
ECHO
SILENT
DREAMS

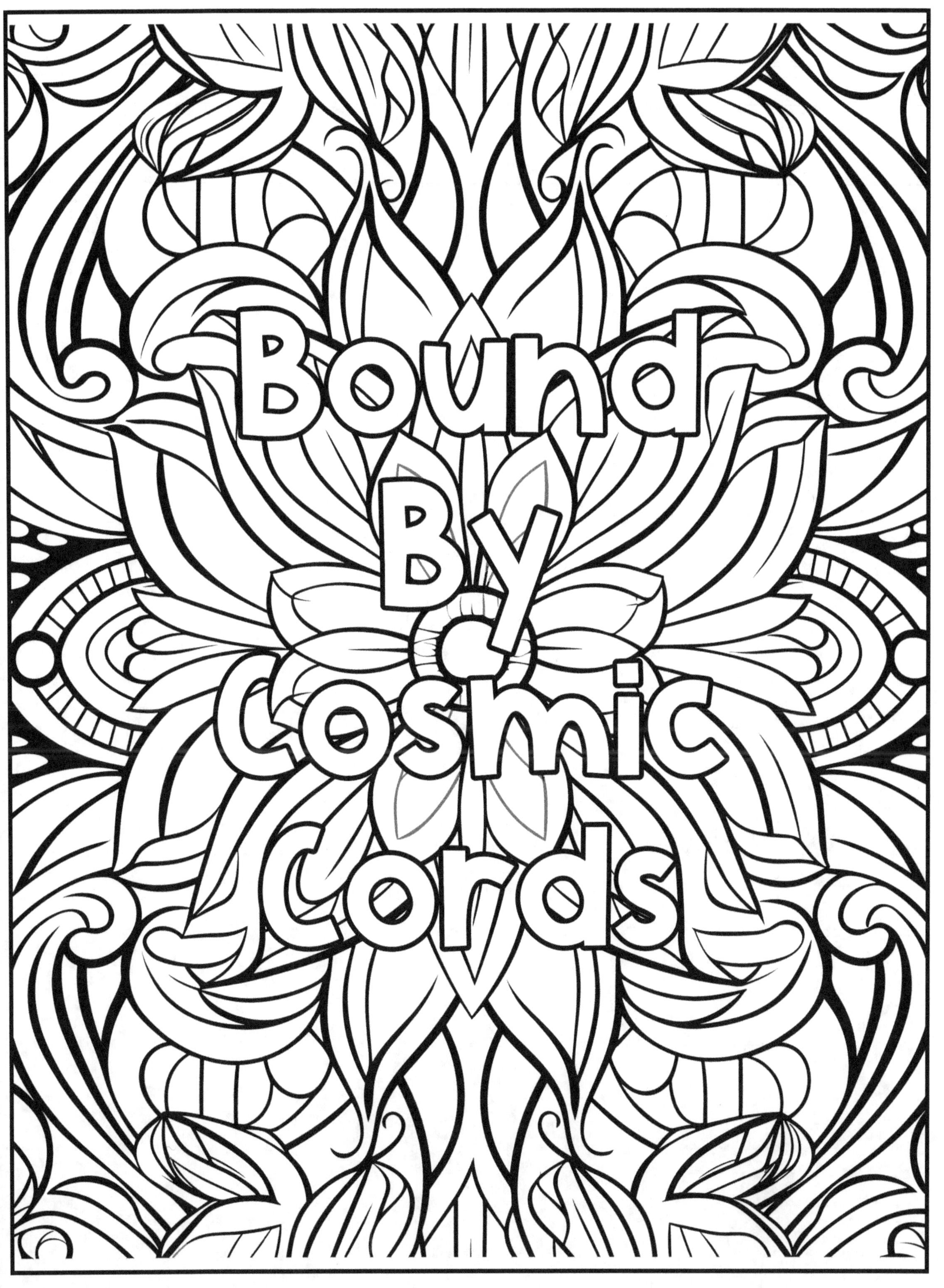

Bound
By
Cosmic
Cords

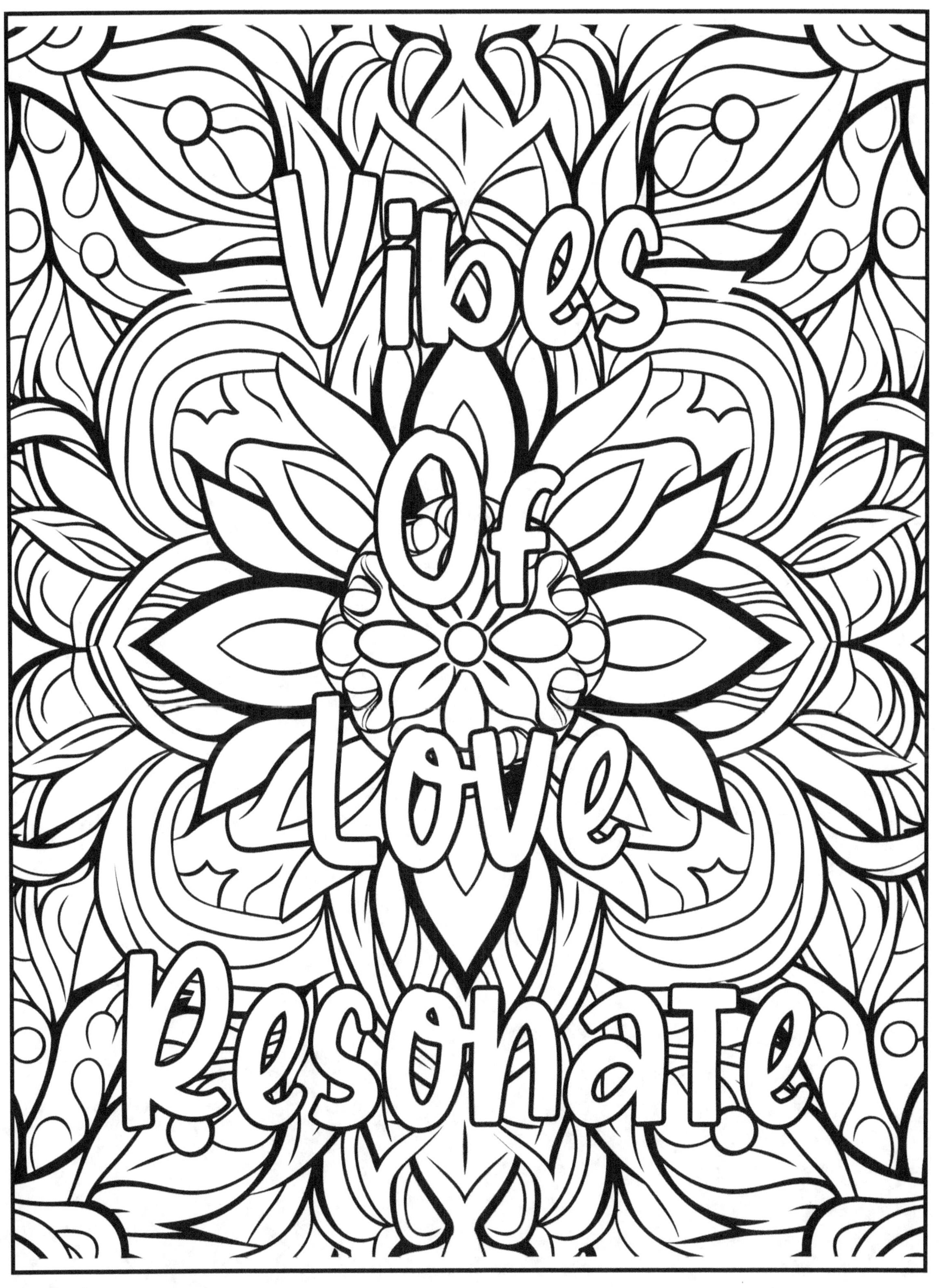

Vibes
Of
Love
Resonate

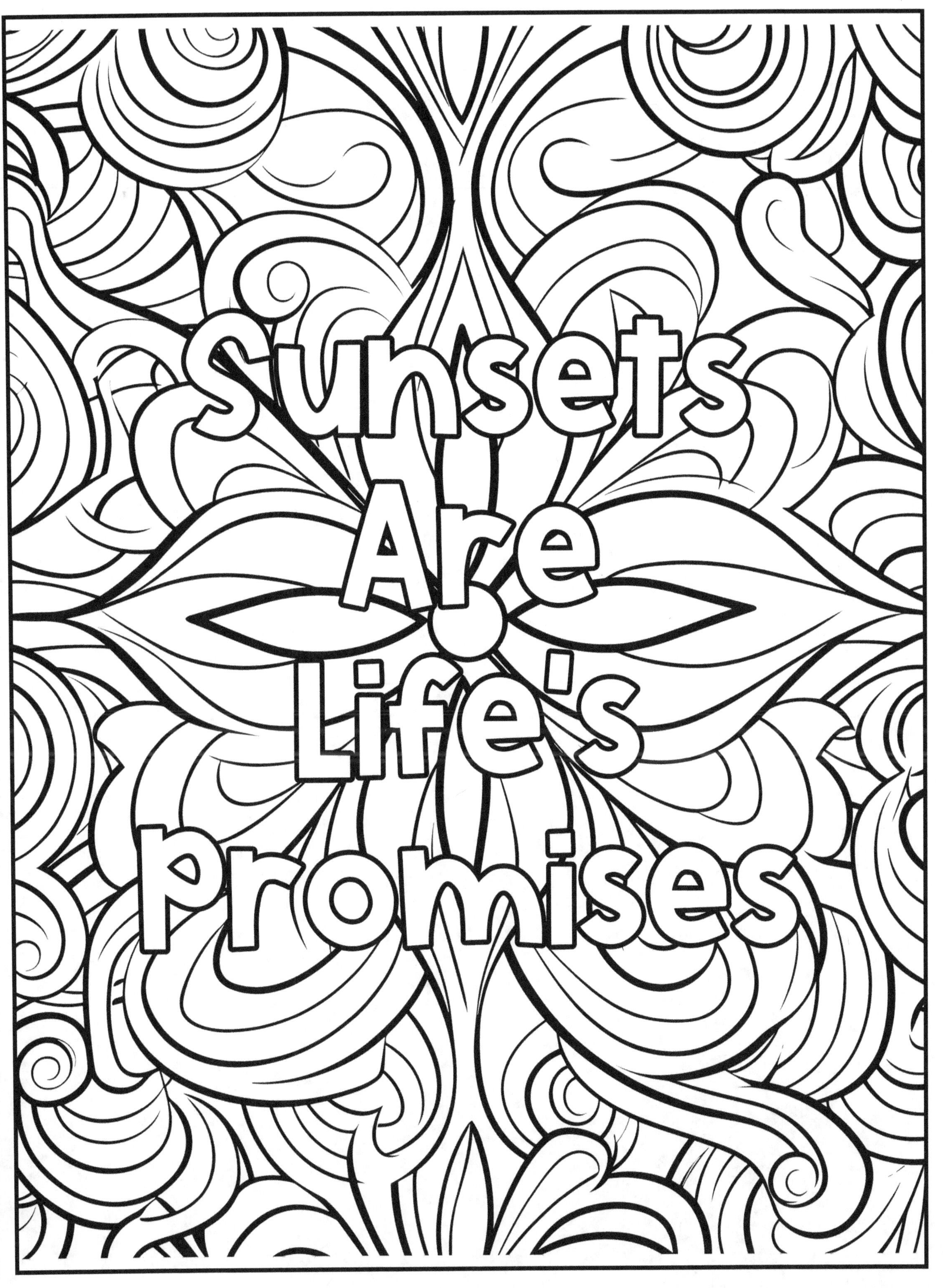

Sunsets
Are
Life's
Promises

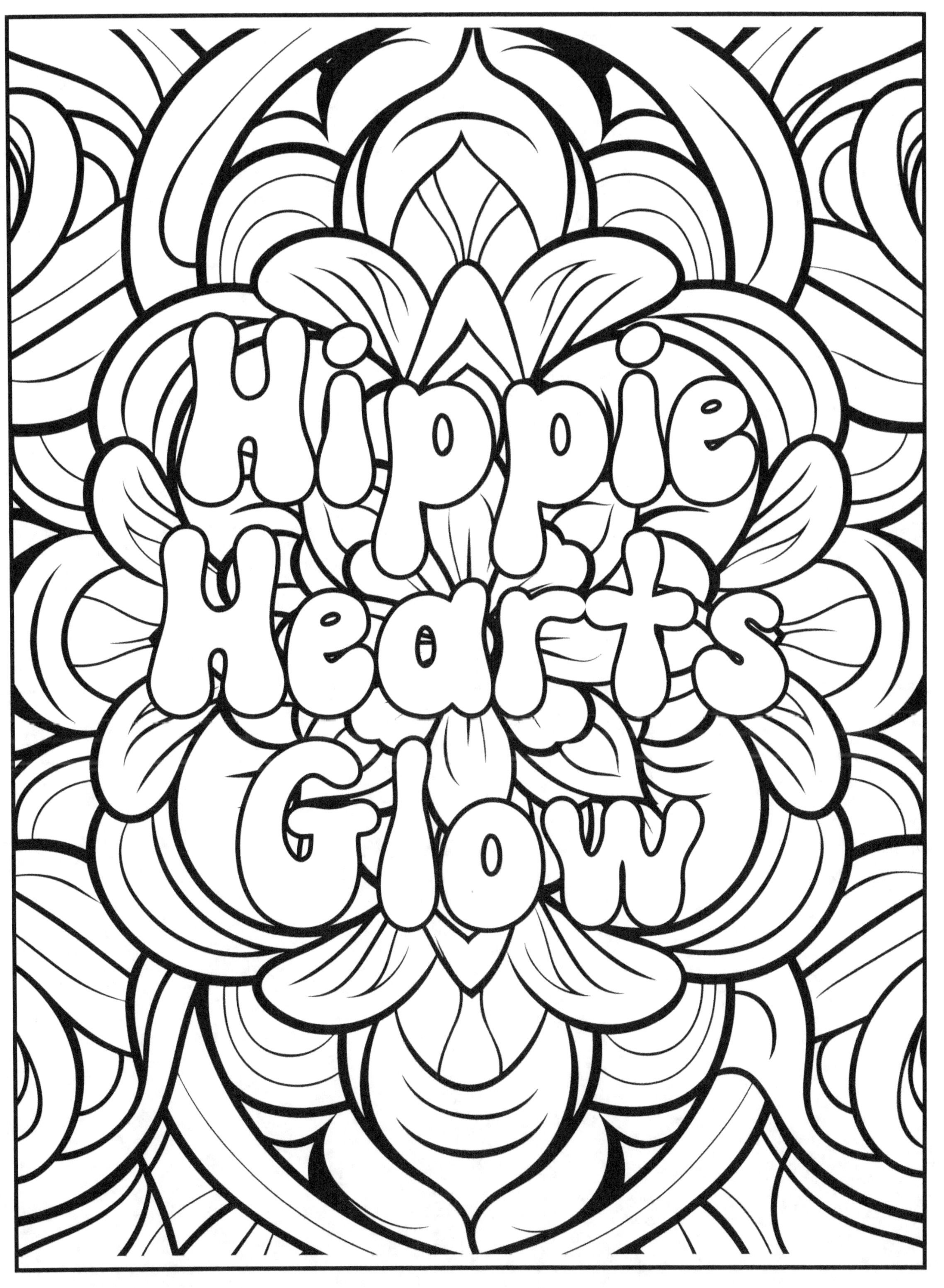

Hippie
Hearts
Glow

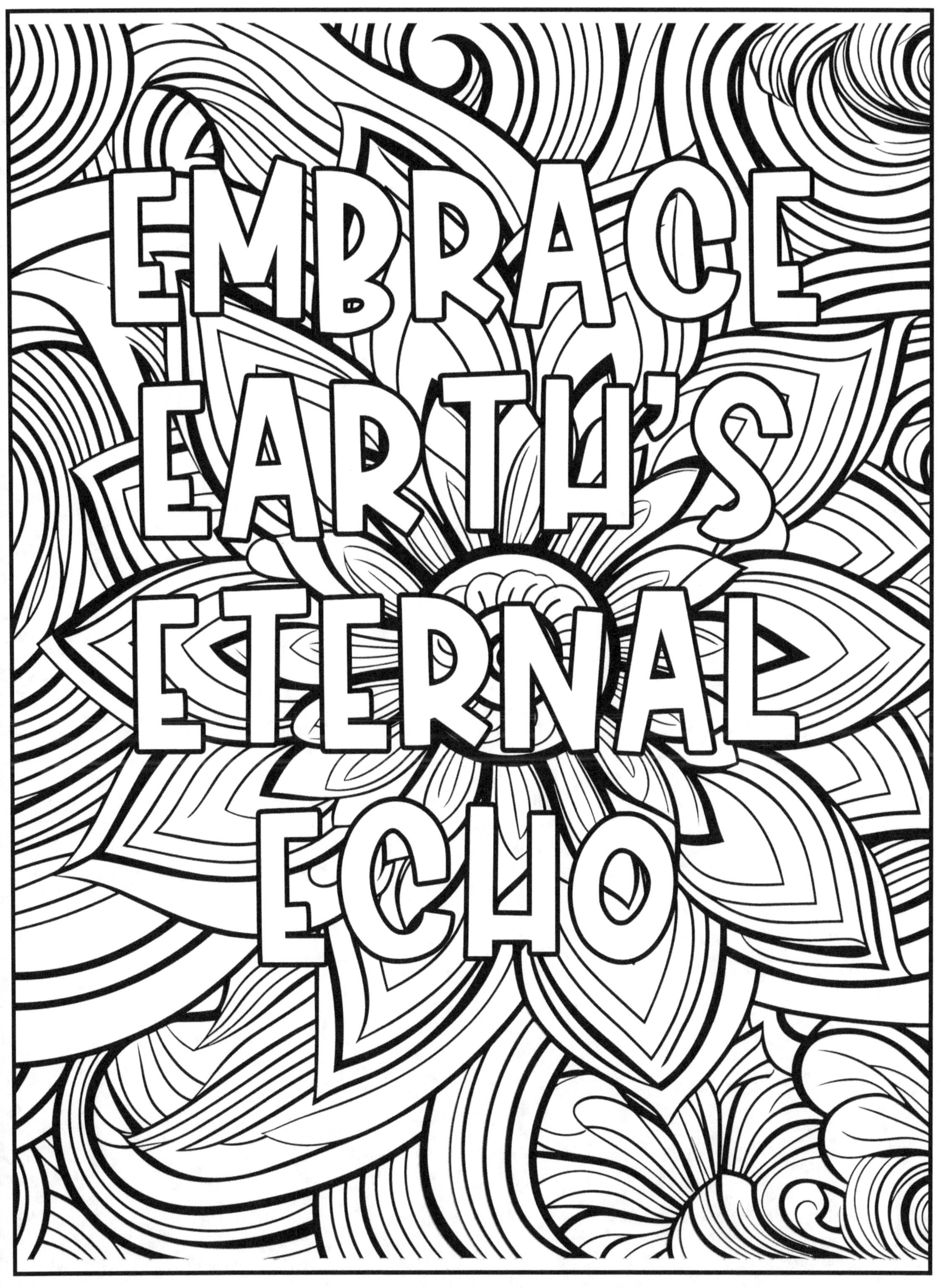

EMBRACE
EARTH'S
ETERNAL
ECHO

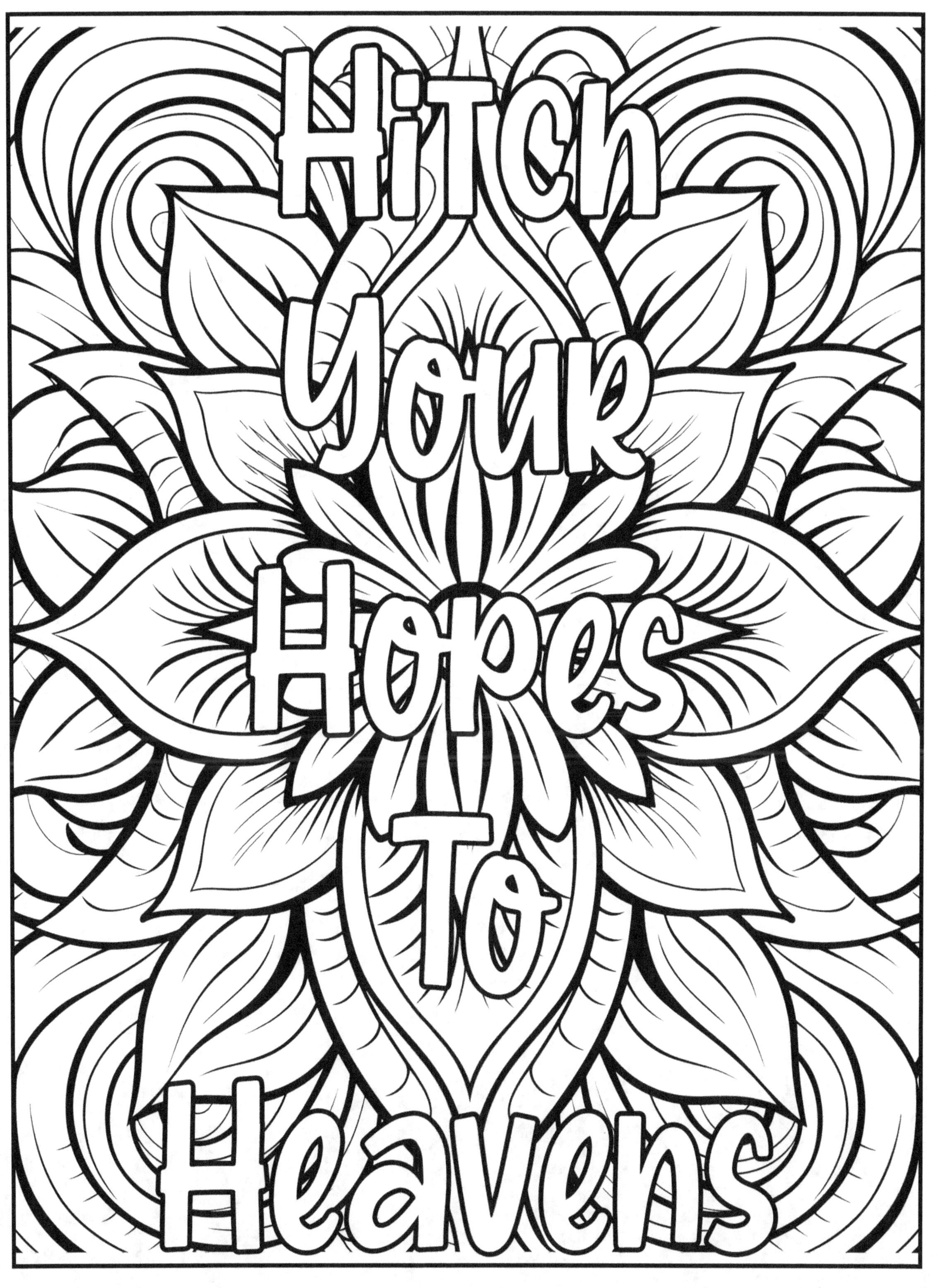
Hitch
Your
Hopes
To
Heavens

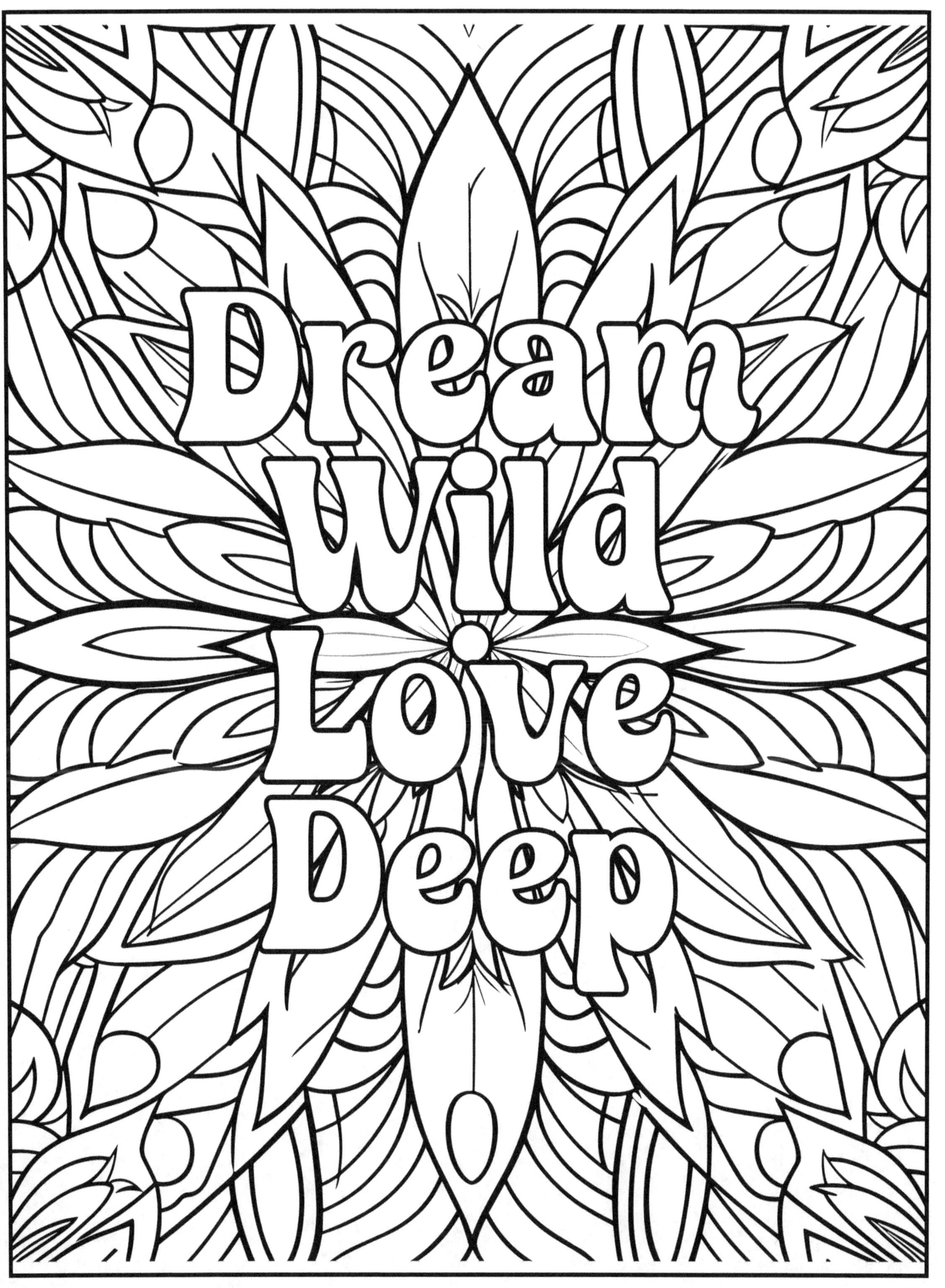

Dream
Wild
Love
Deep

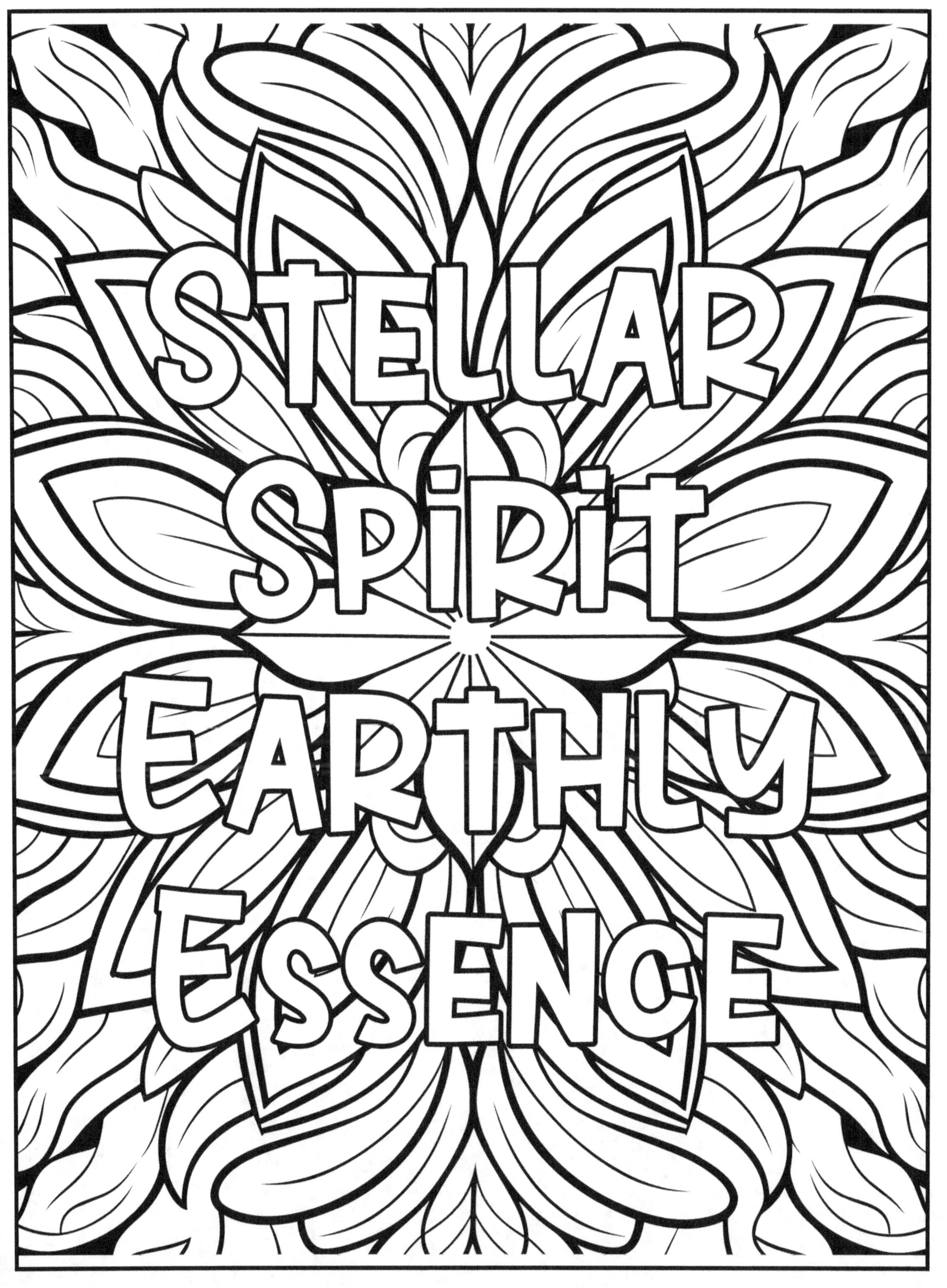
STELLAR
SPIRIT
EARTHLY
ESSENCE

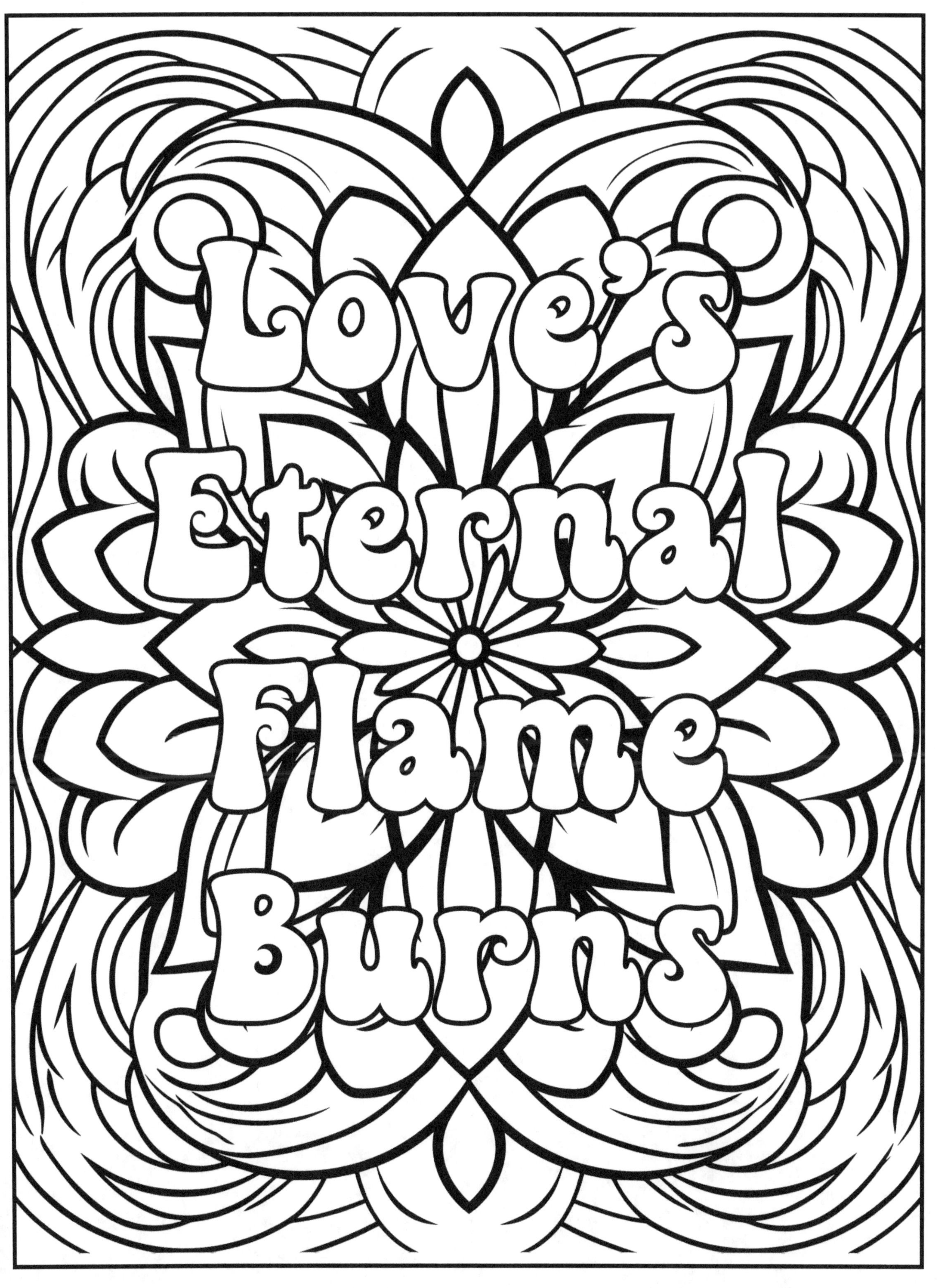

Love's
Eternal
Flame
Burns

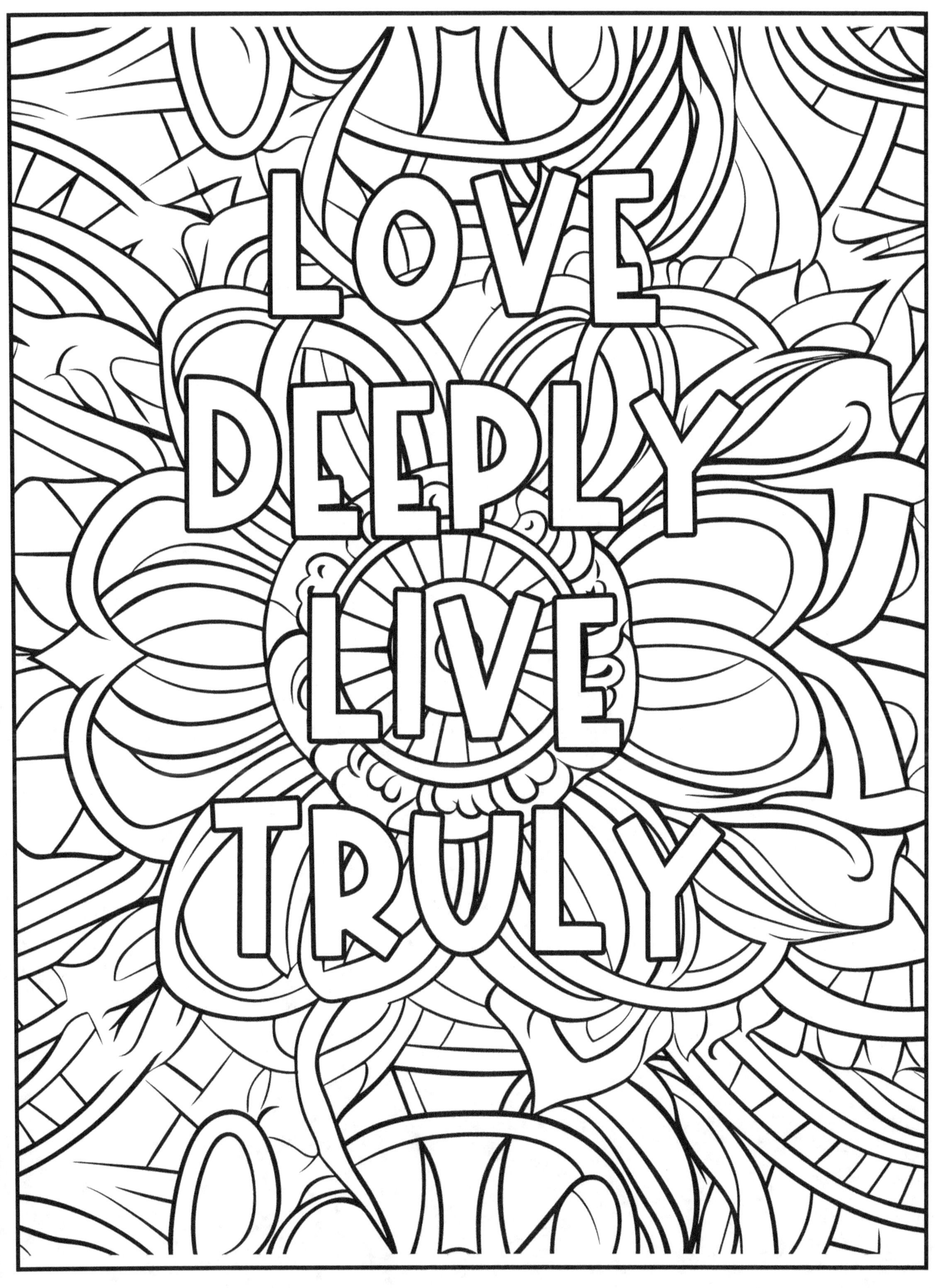

LOVE
DEEPLY
LIVE
TRULY

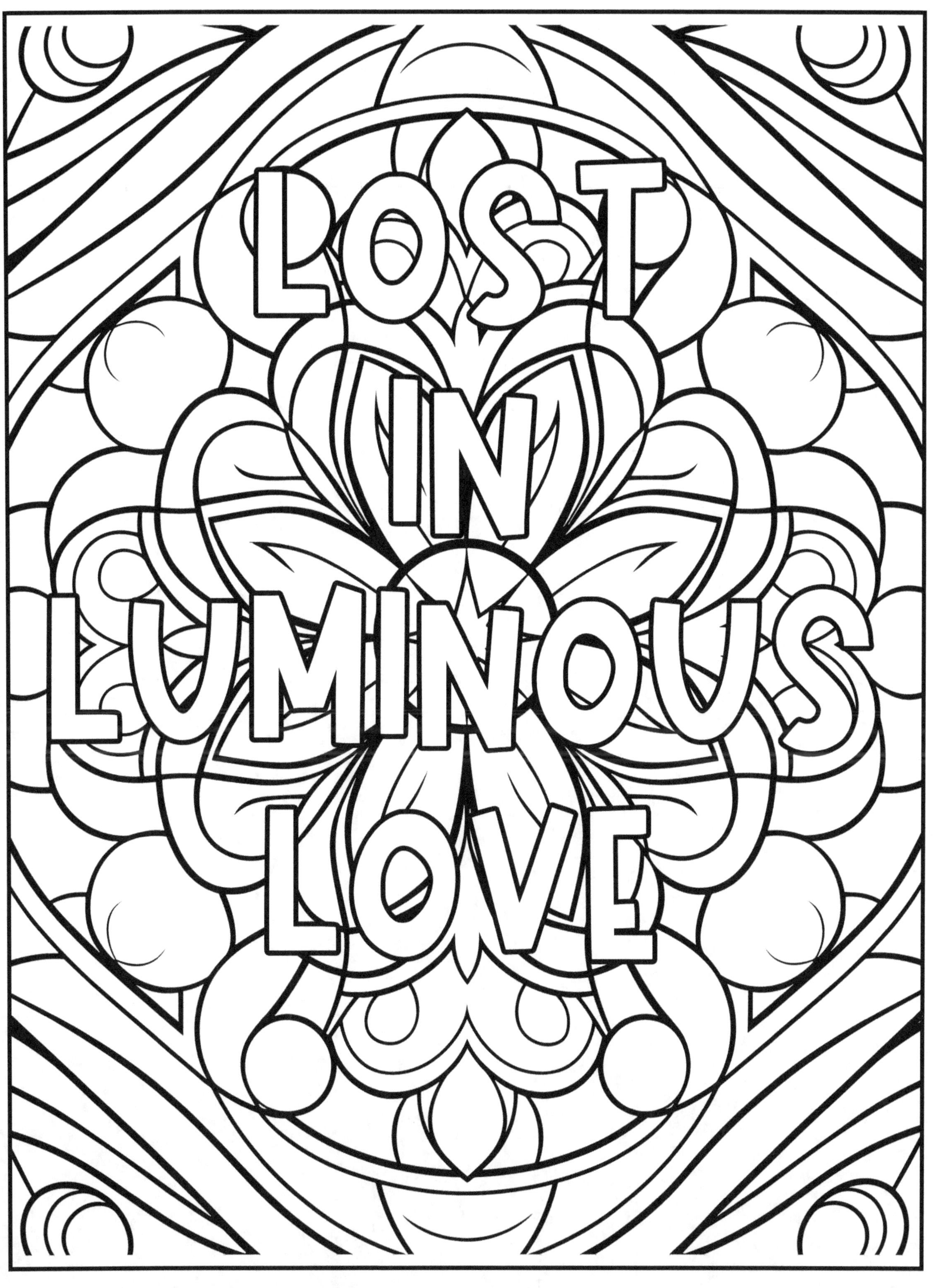

LOST
IN
LUMINOUS
LOVE

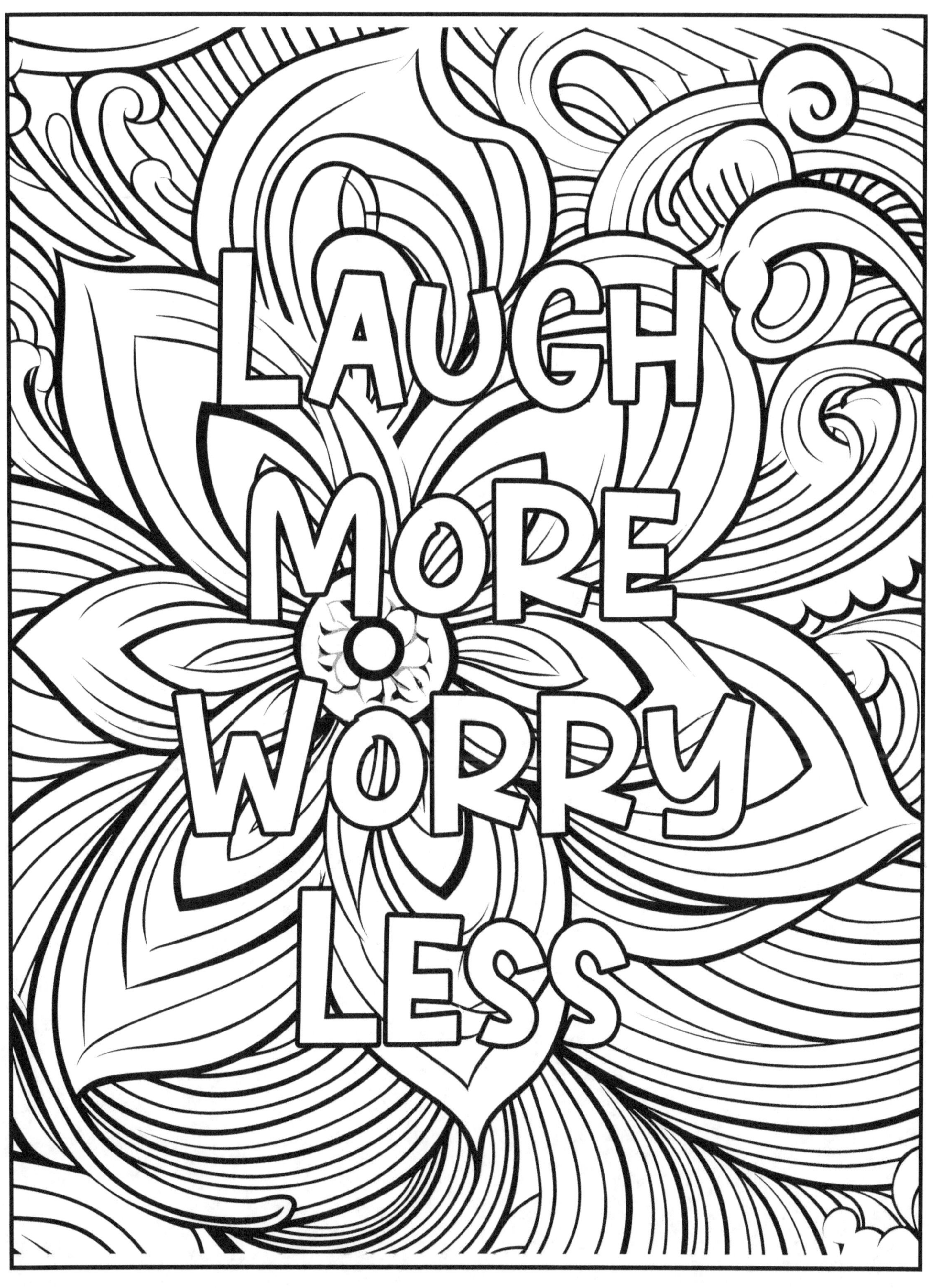

Laugh
More
Worry
Less

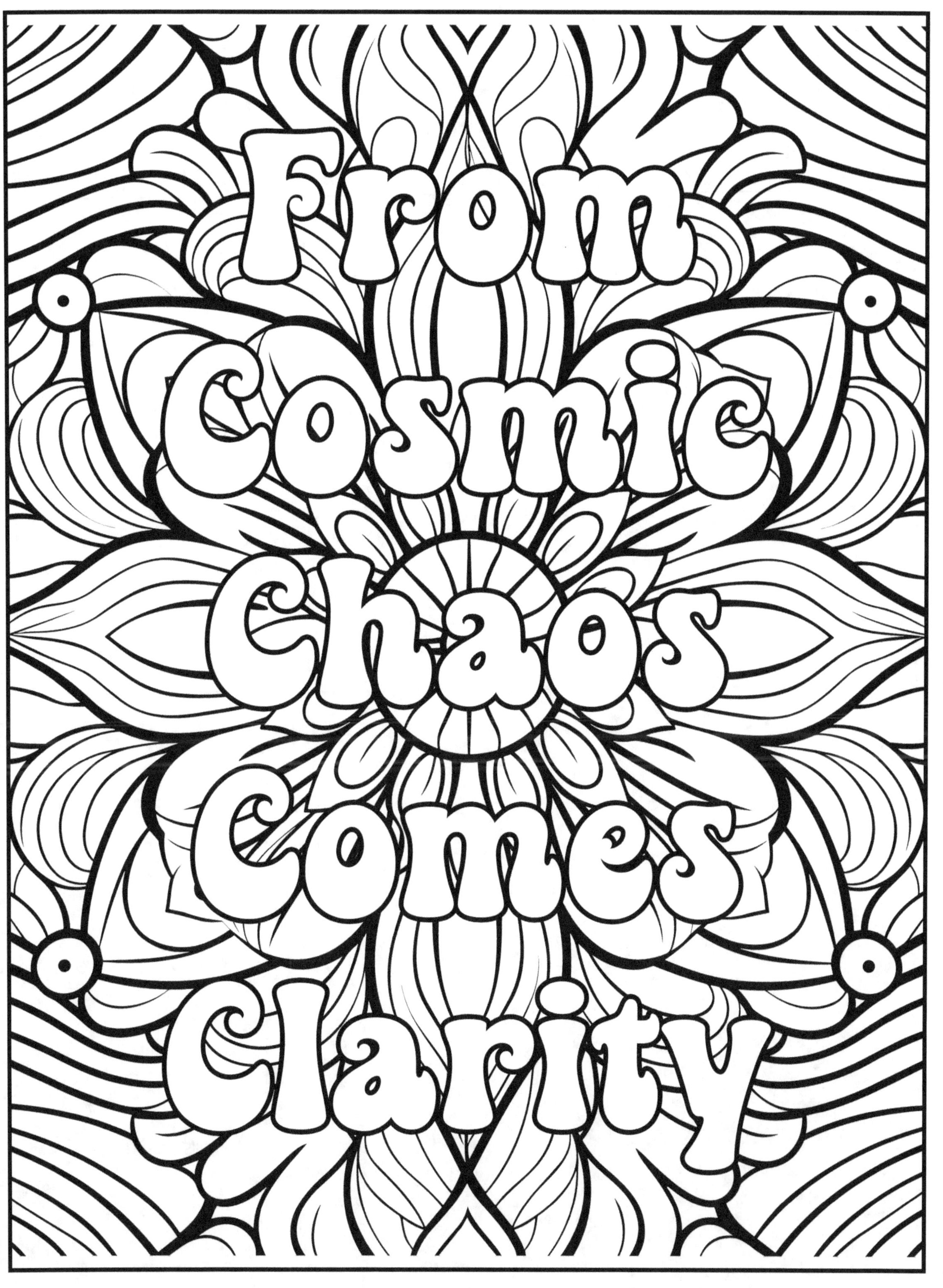

From
Cosmic
Chaos
Comes
Clarity

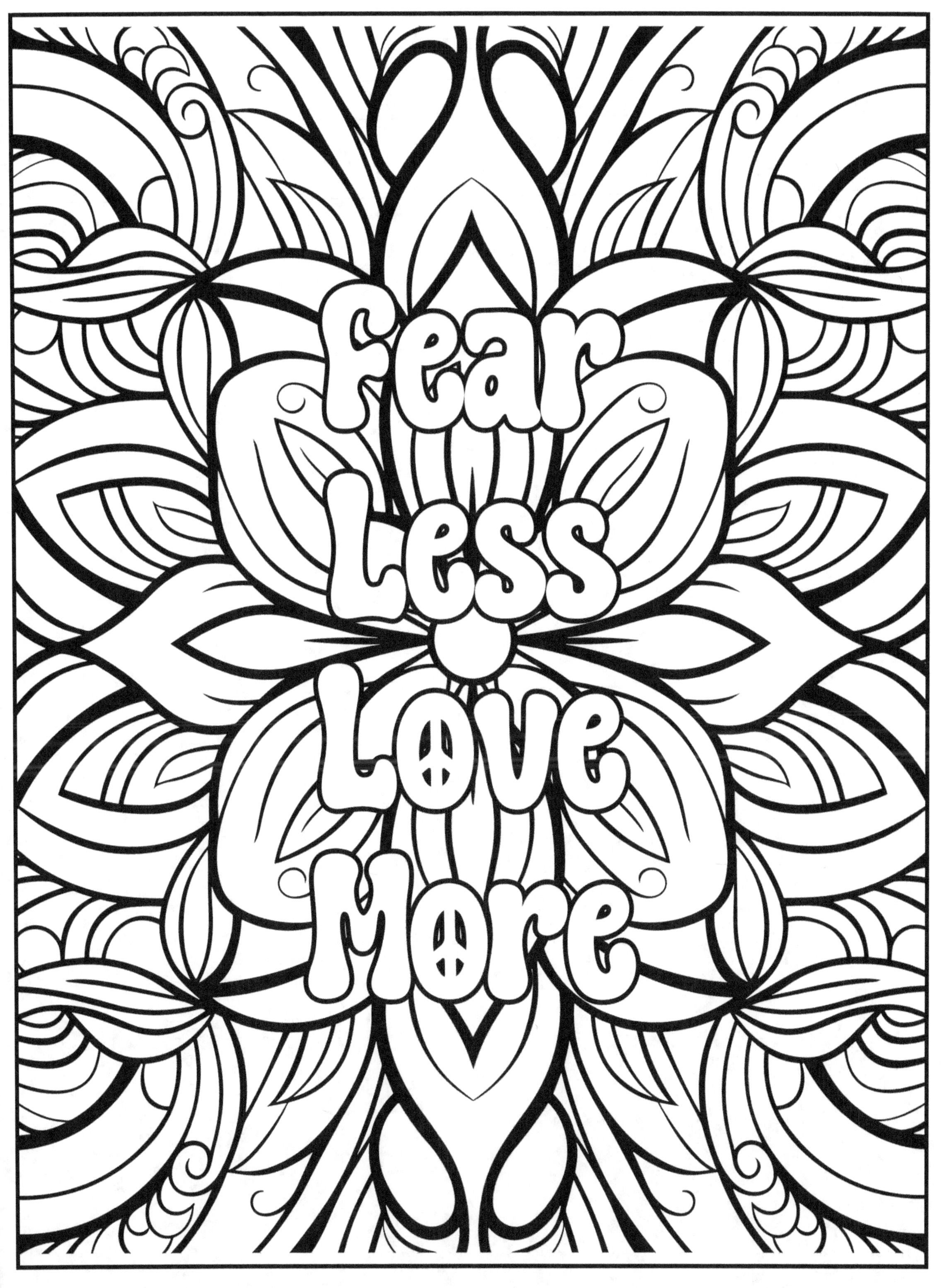

Fear
Less
Love
More

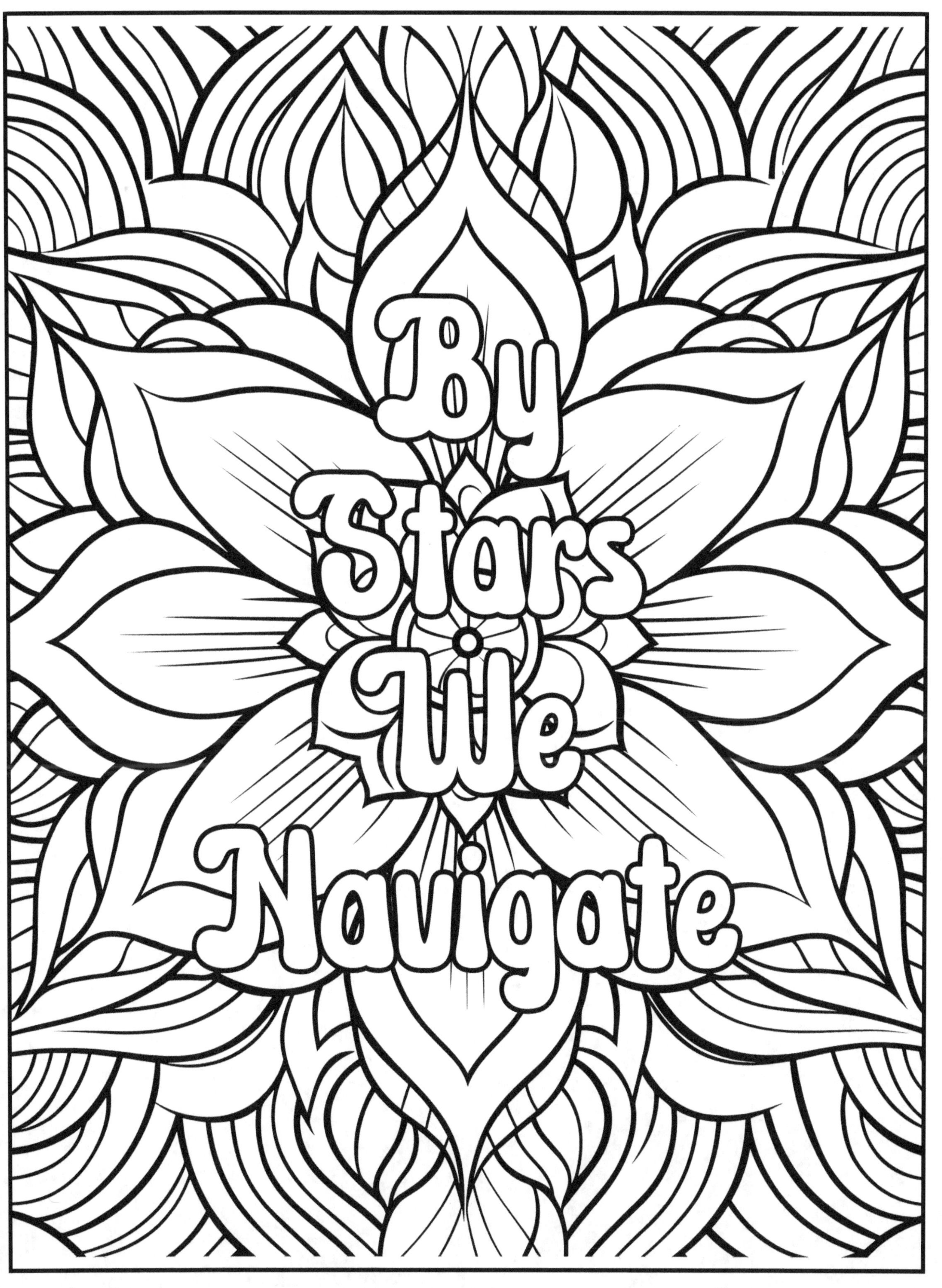
By
Stars
We
Navigate

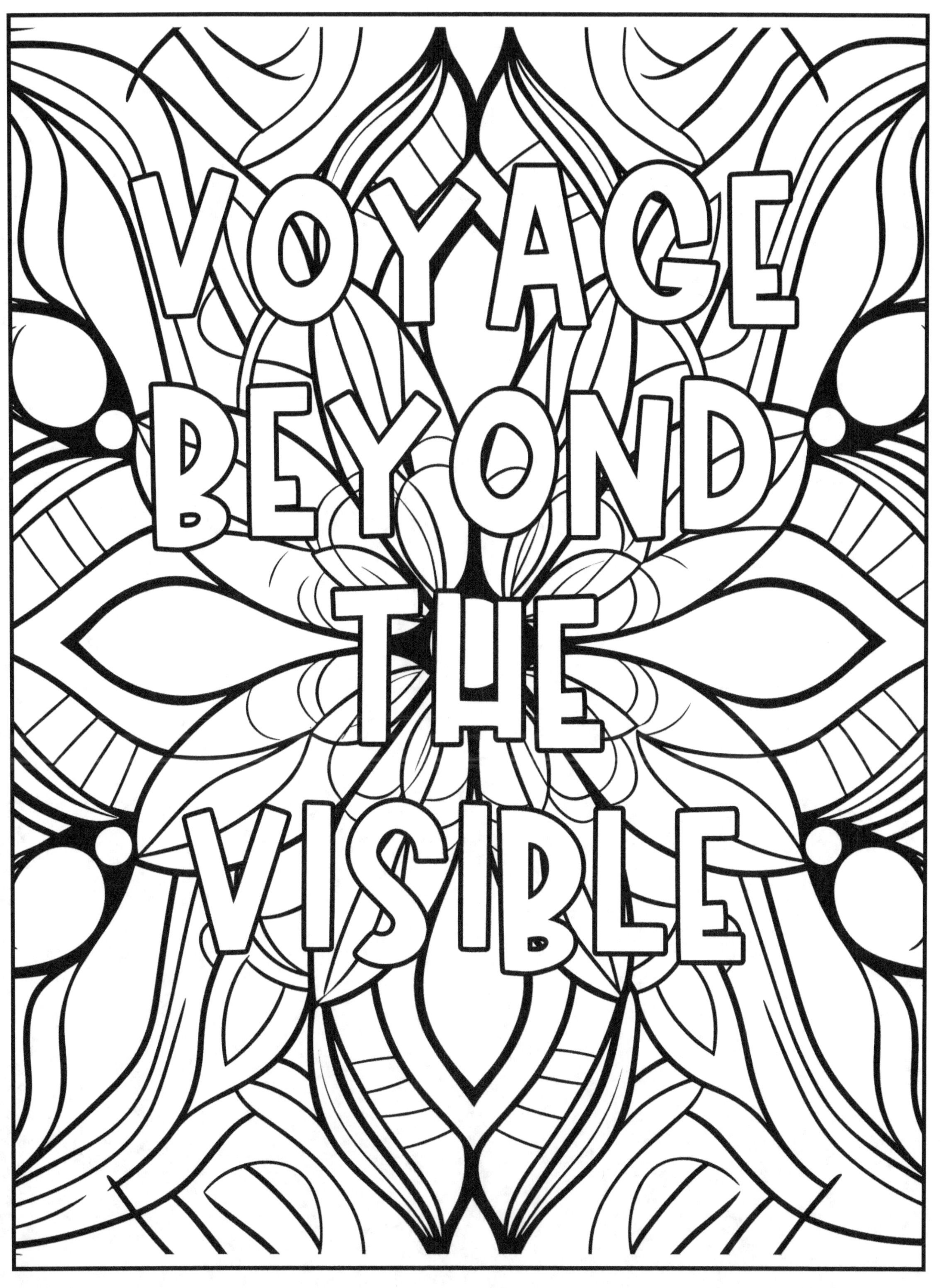
VOYAGE
BEYOND
THE
VISIBLE

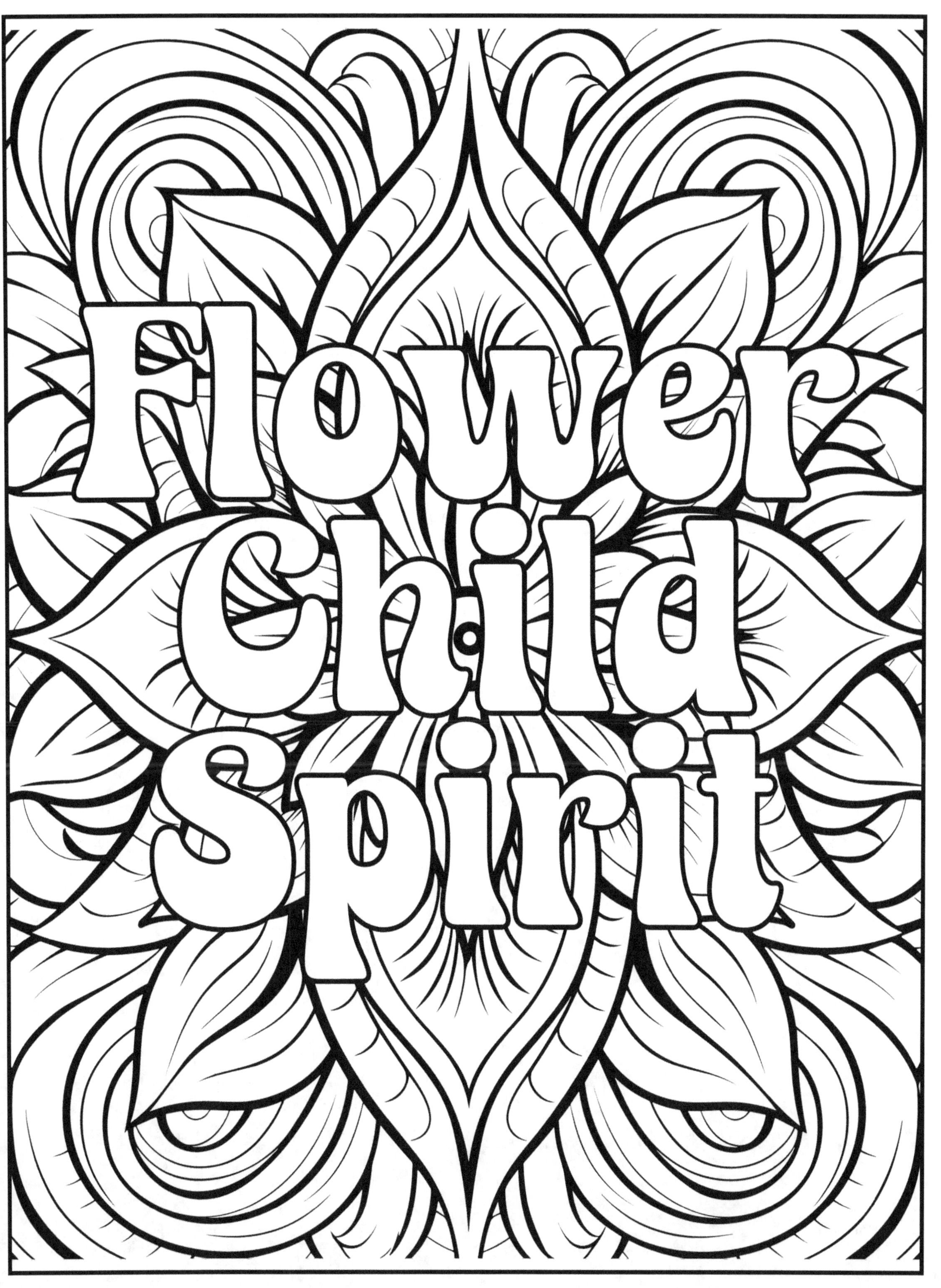
Flower
Child
Spirit

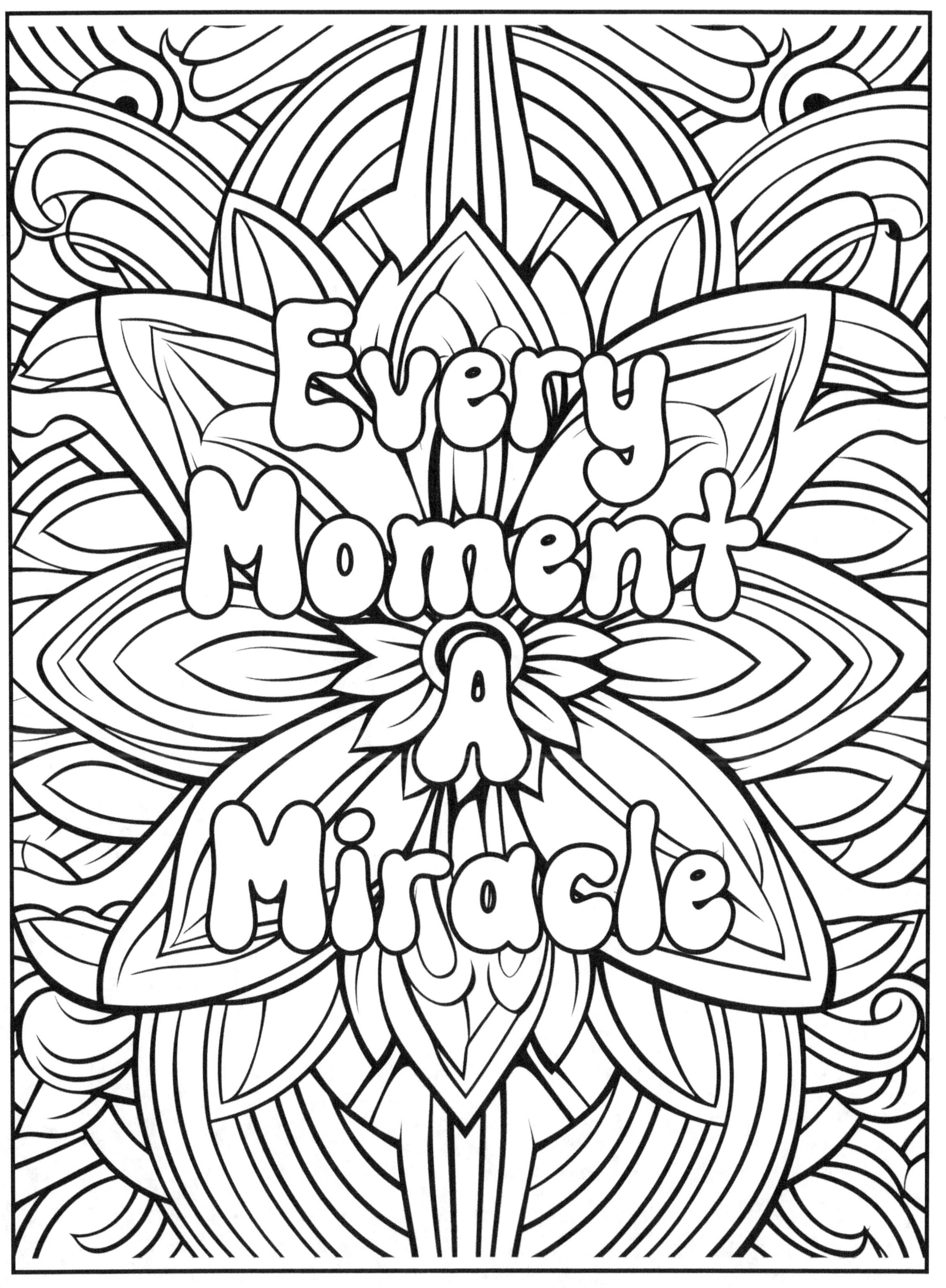

Every
Moment
A
Miracle

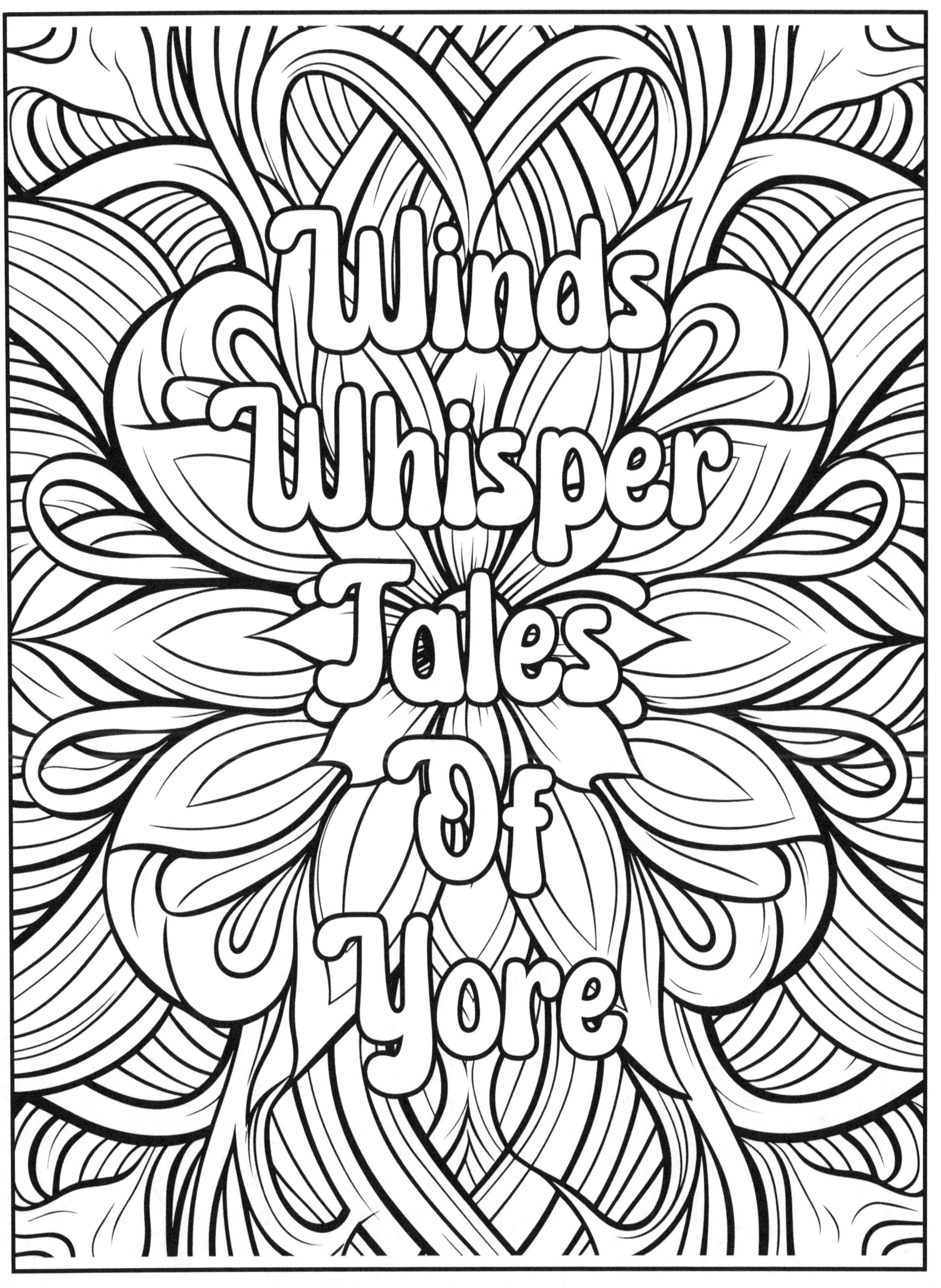

Winds
Whisper
Tales
Of
Yore

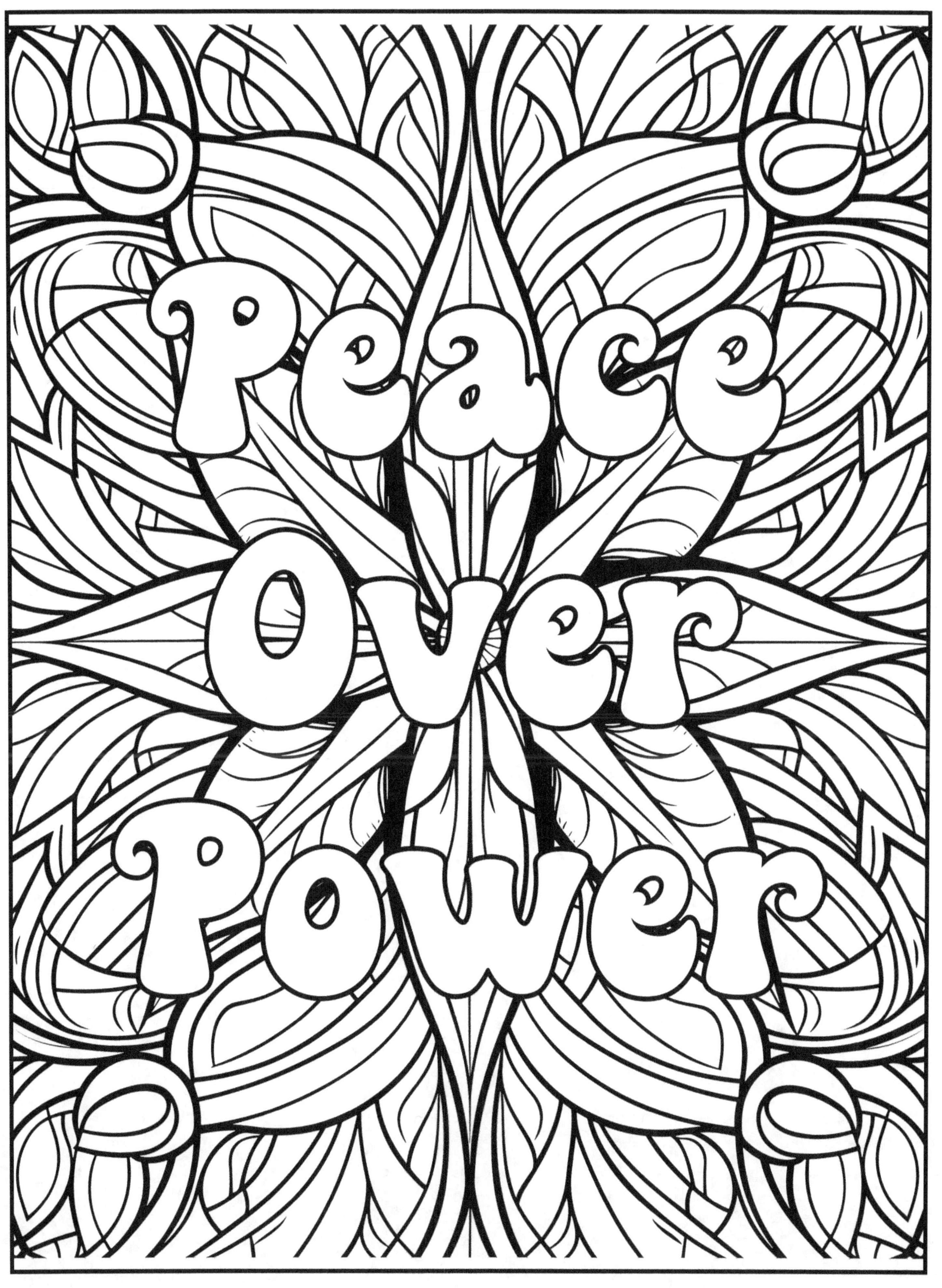

Peace
Over
Power

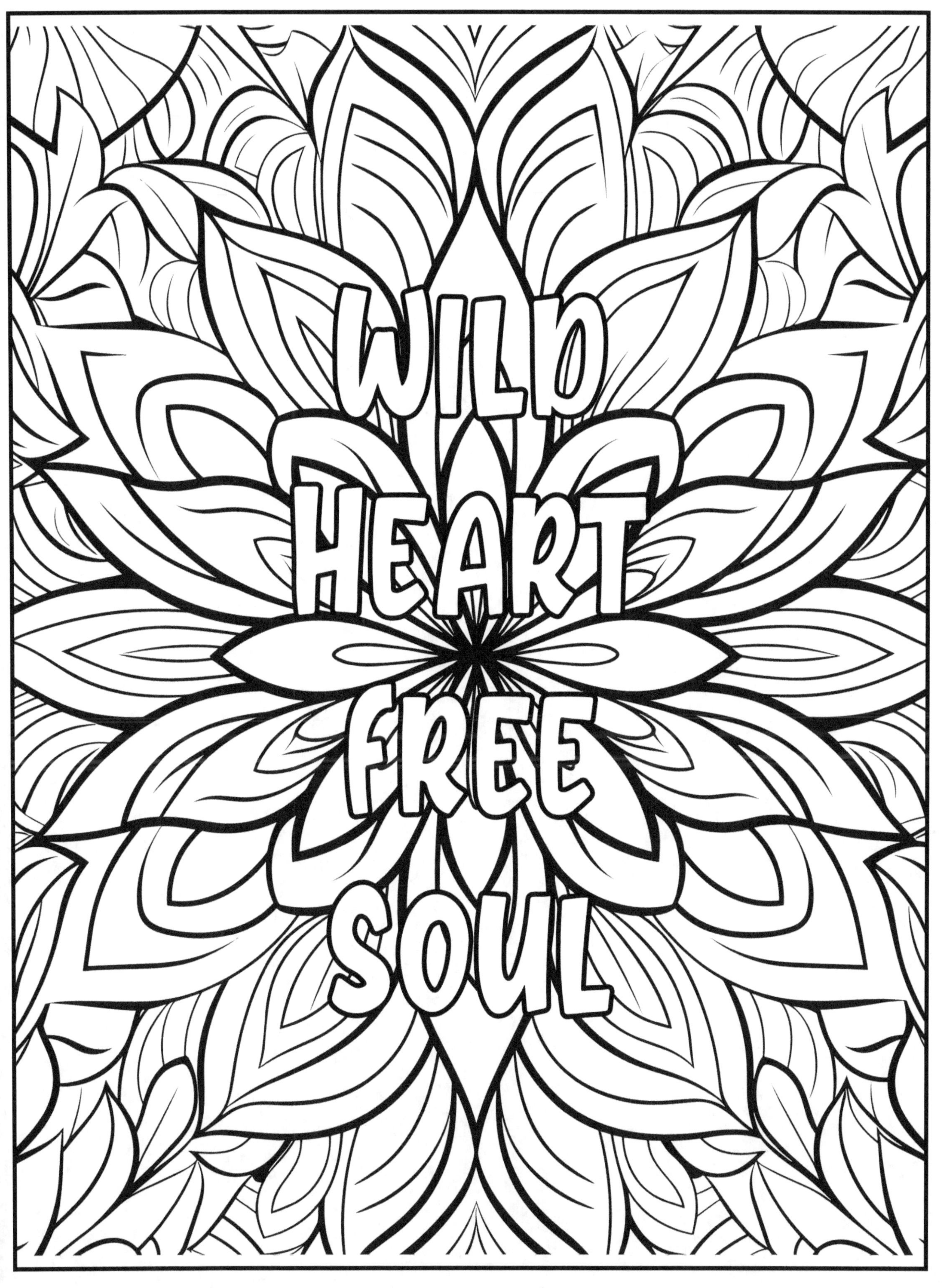

WILD
HEART
FREE
SOUL

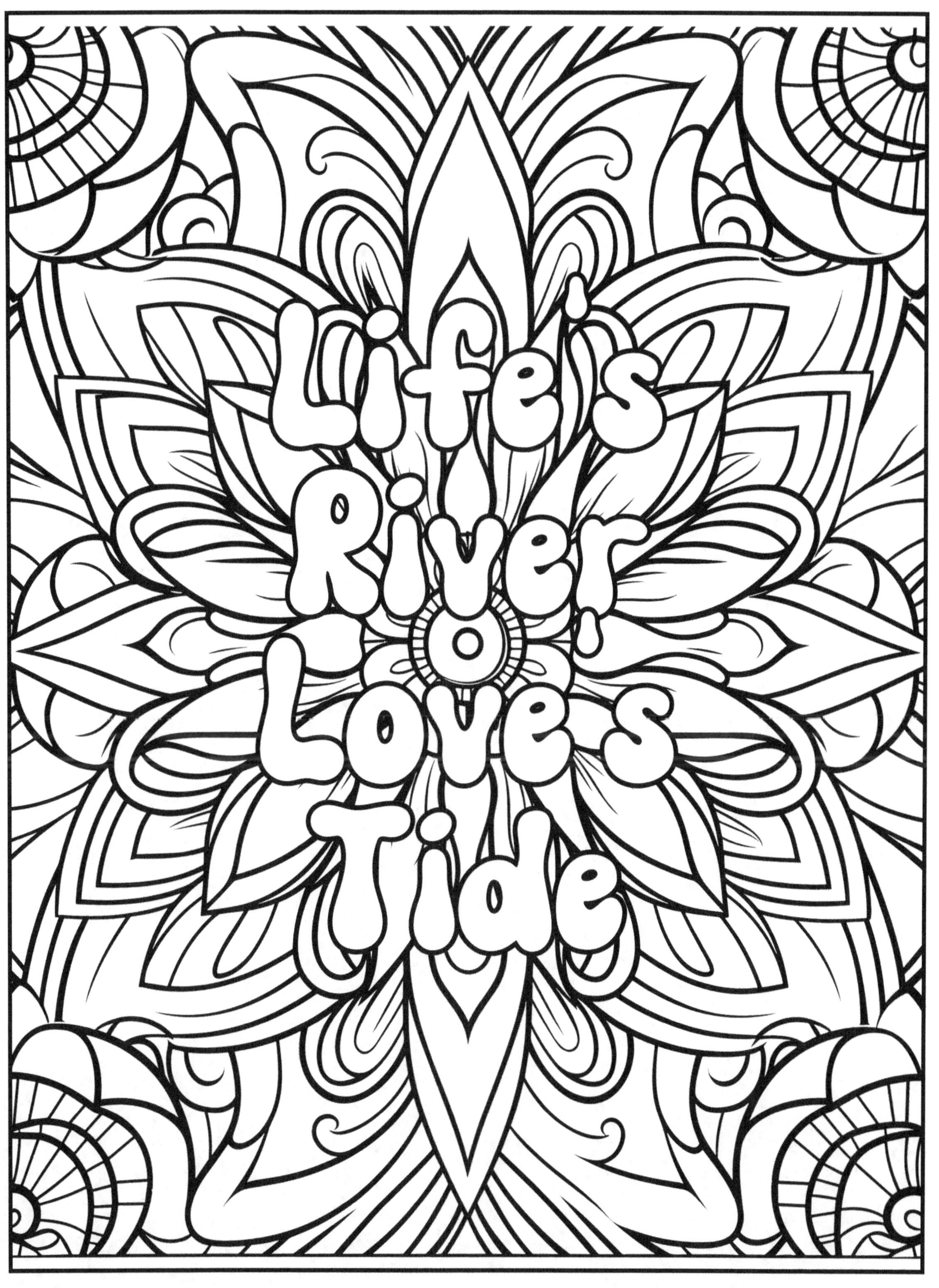

Life's
River
Love's
Tide

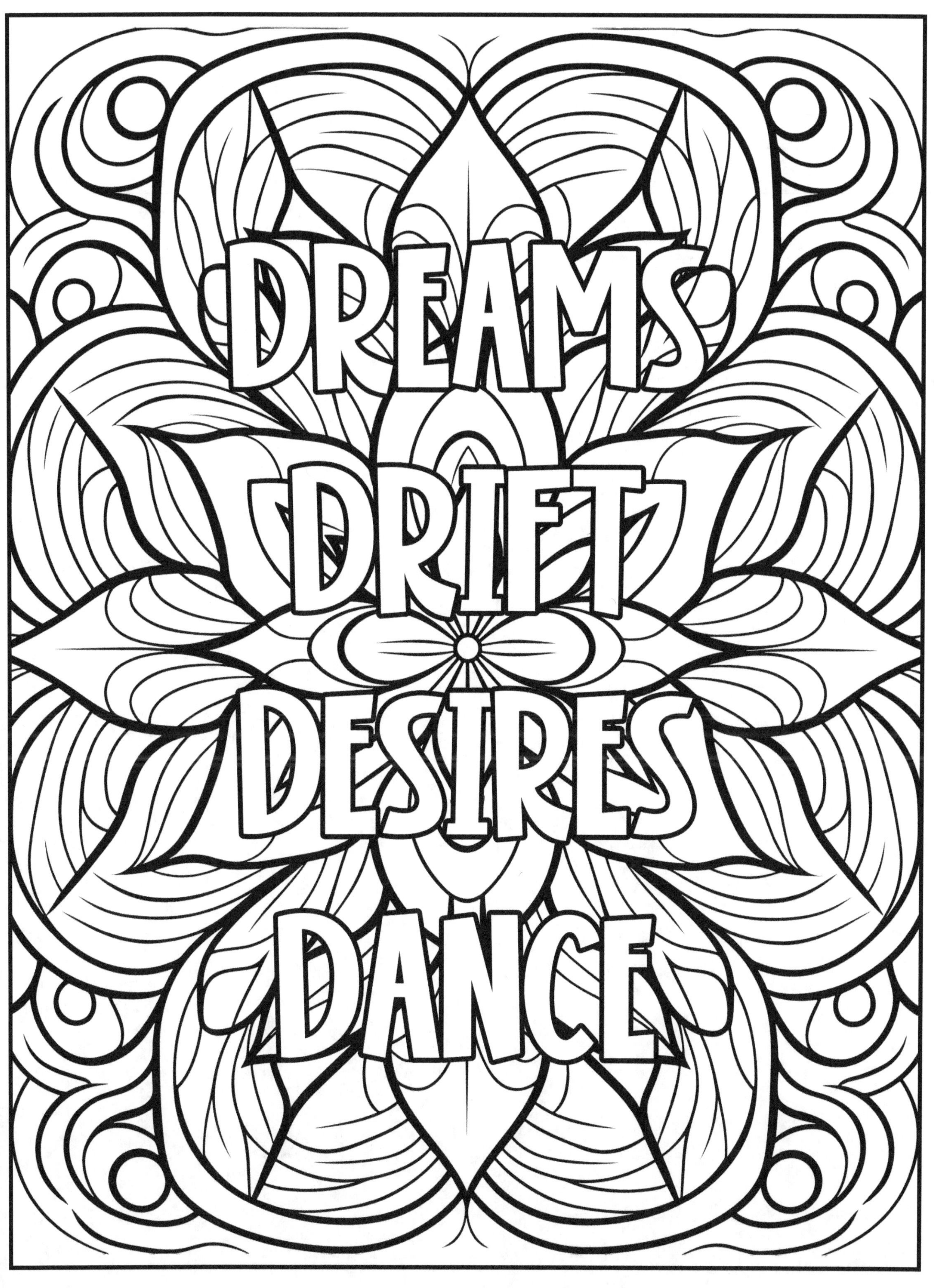

DREAMS
DRIFT
DESIRES
DANCE

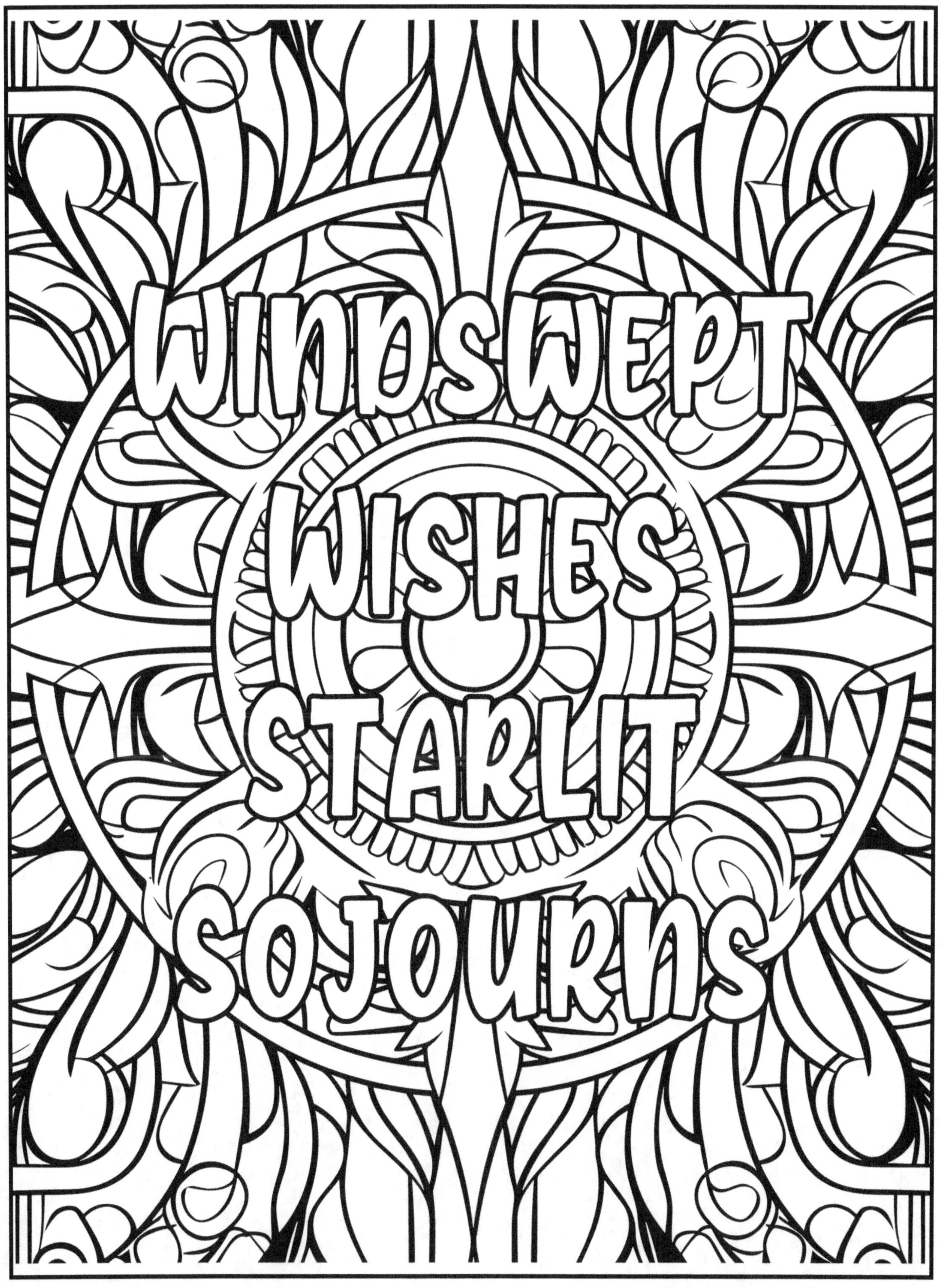

WINDSWEPT
WISHES
STARLIT
SOJOURNS

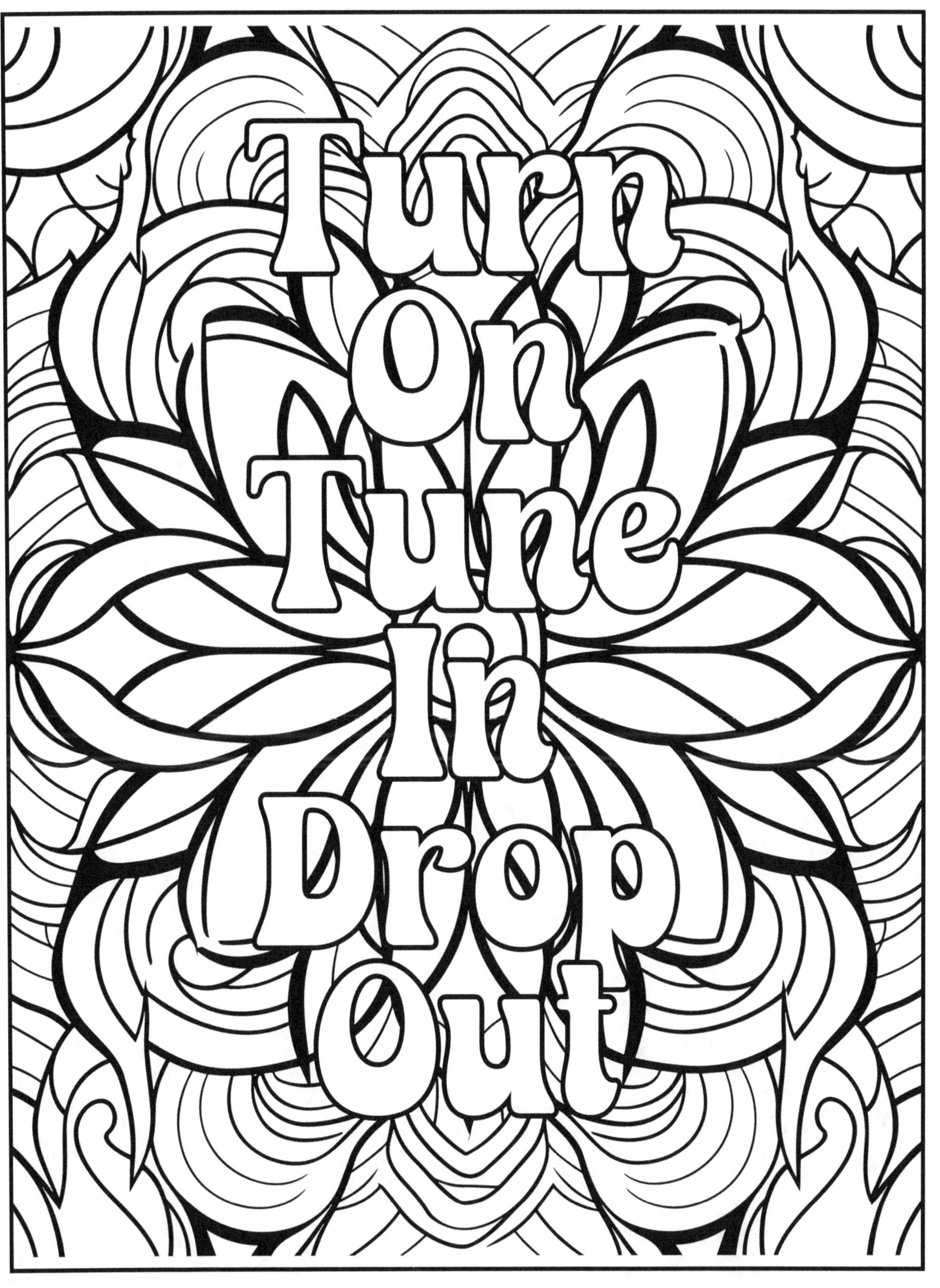

Turn
On
Tune
In
Drop
Out

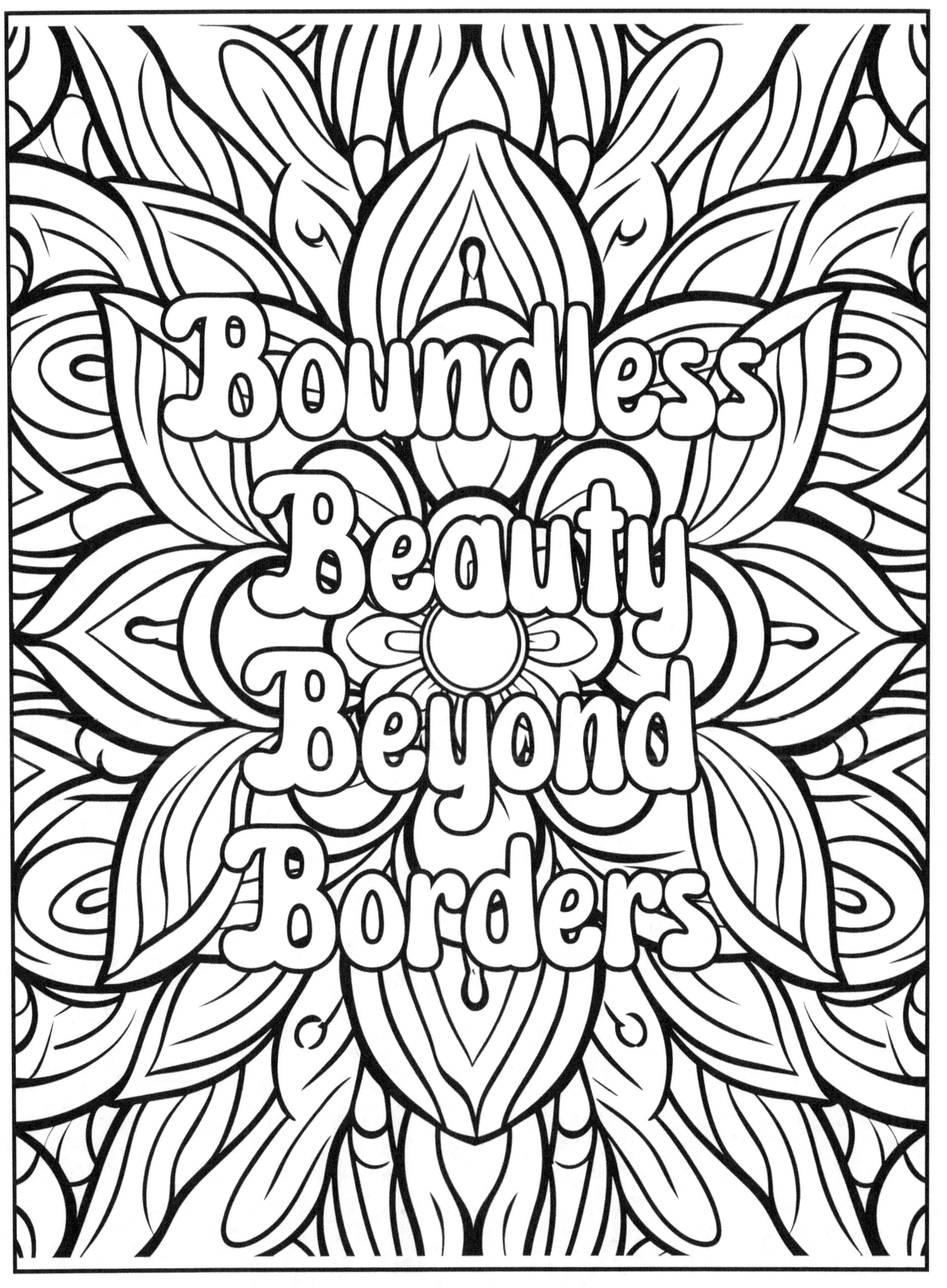
Boundless
Beauty
Beyond
Borders

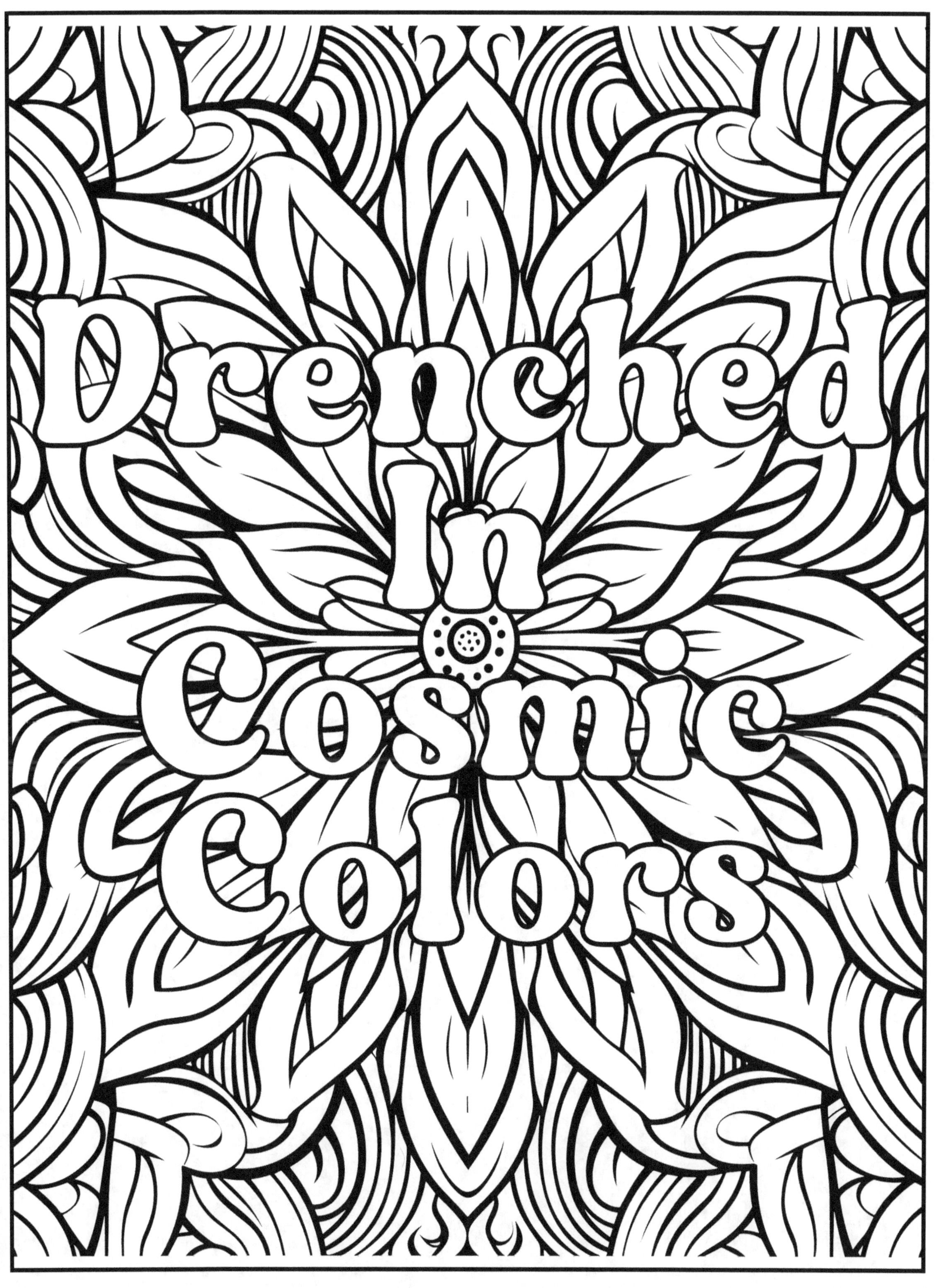

Drenched
In
Cosmic
Colors

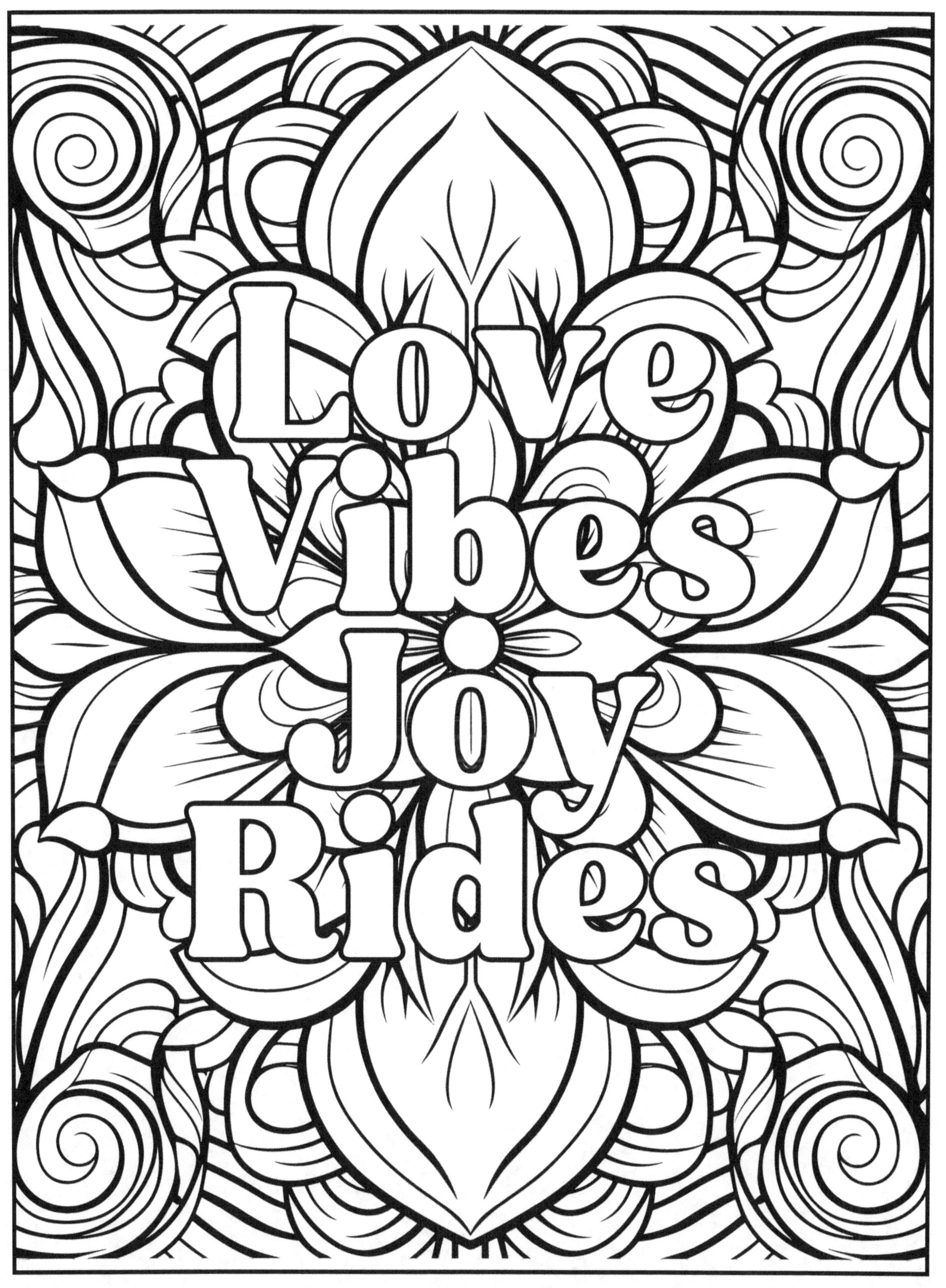

Love
Vibes
Joy
Rides

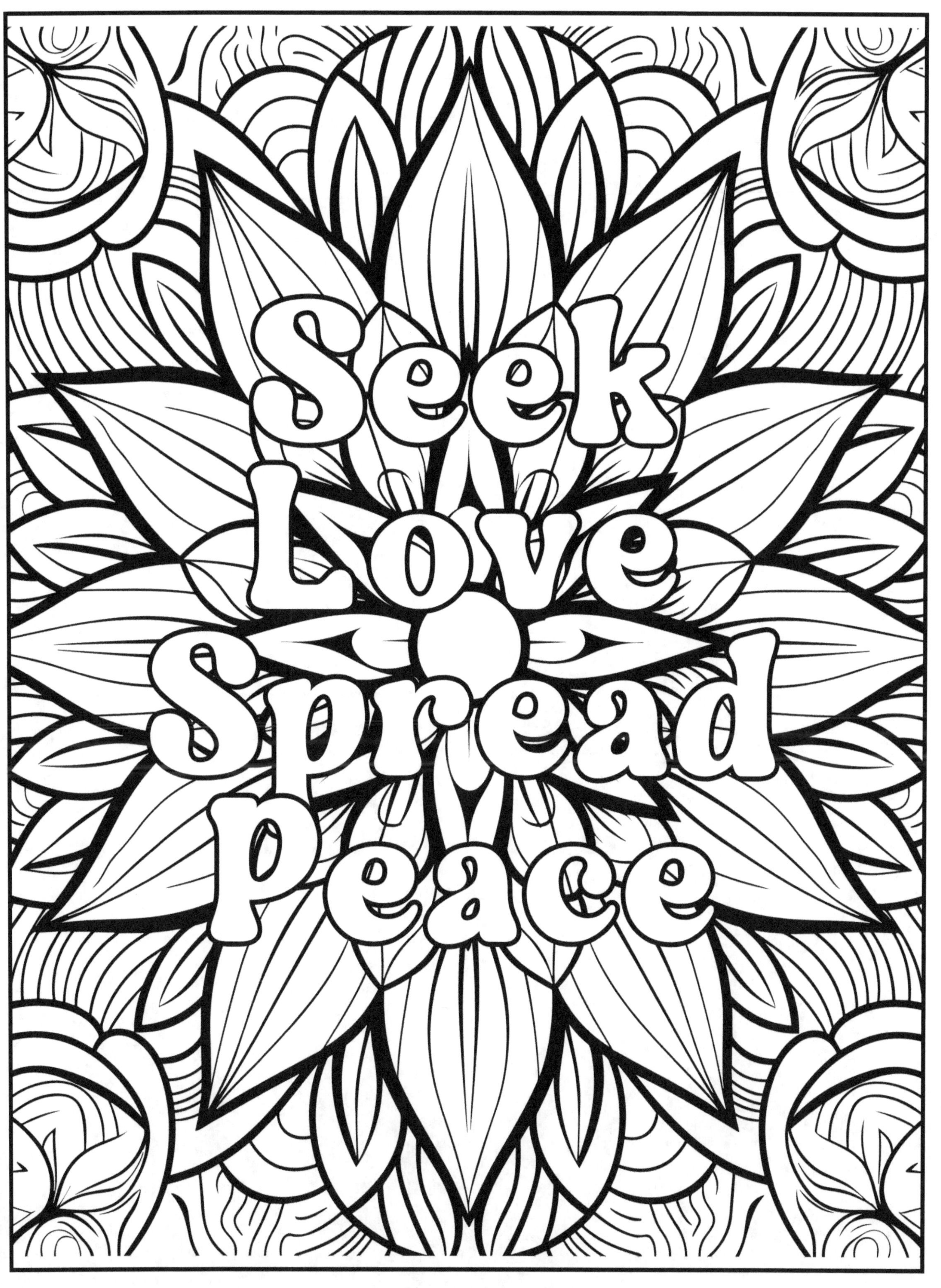
Seek
Love
Spread
peace

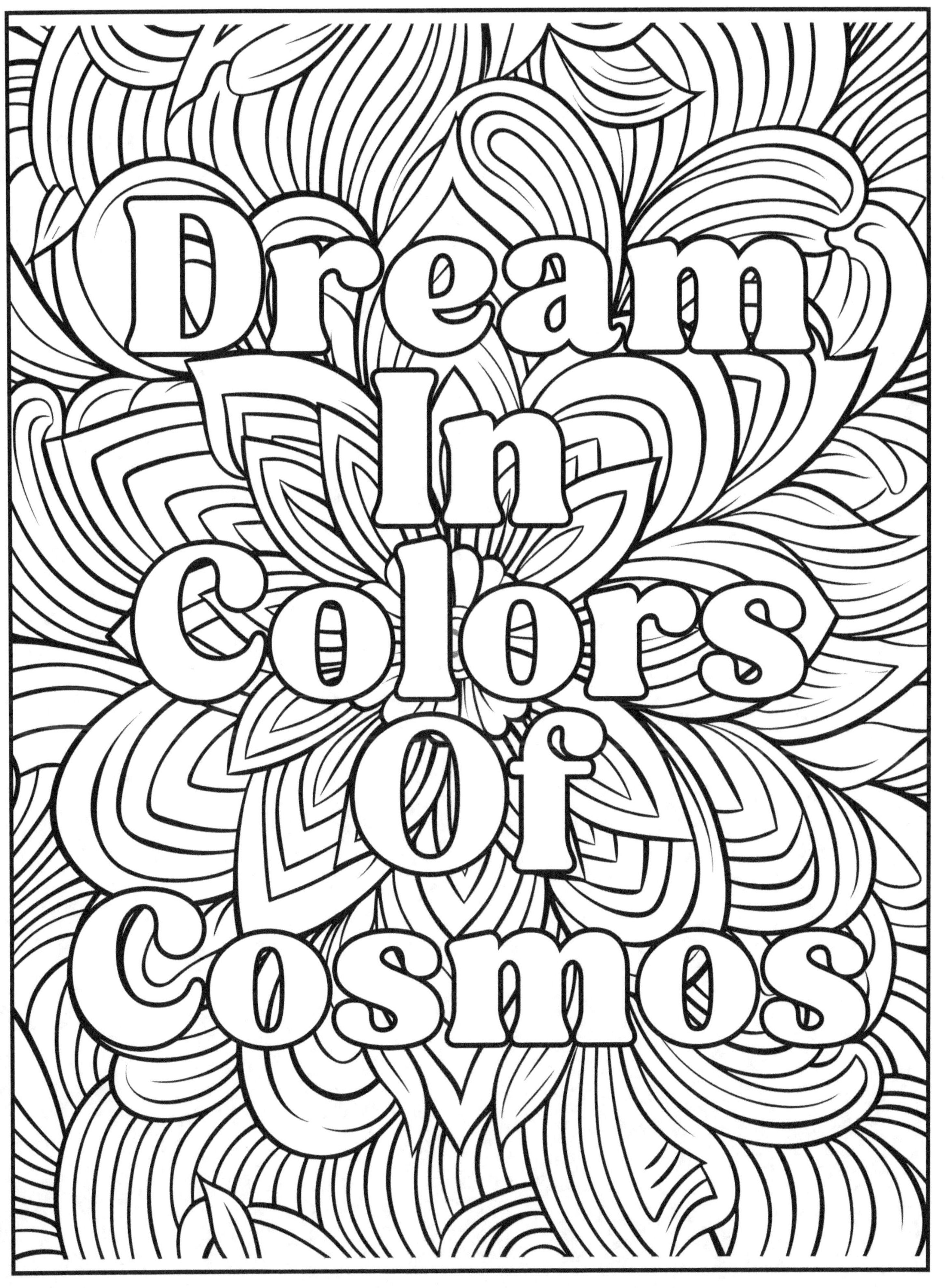

Dream
In
Colors
Of
Cosmos

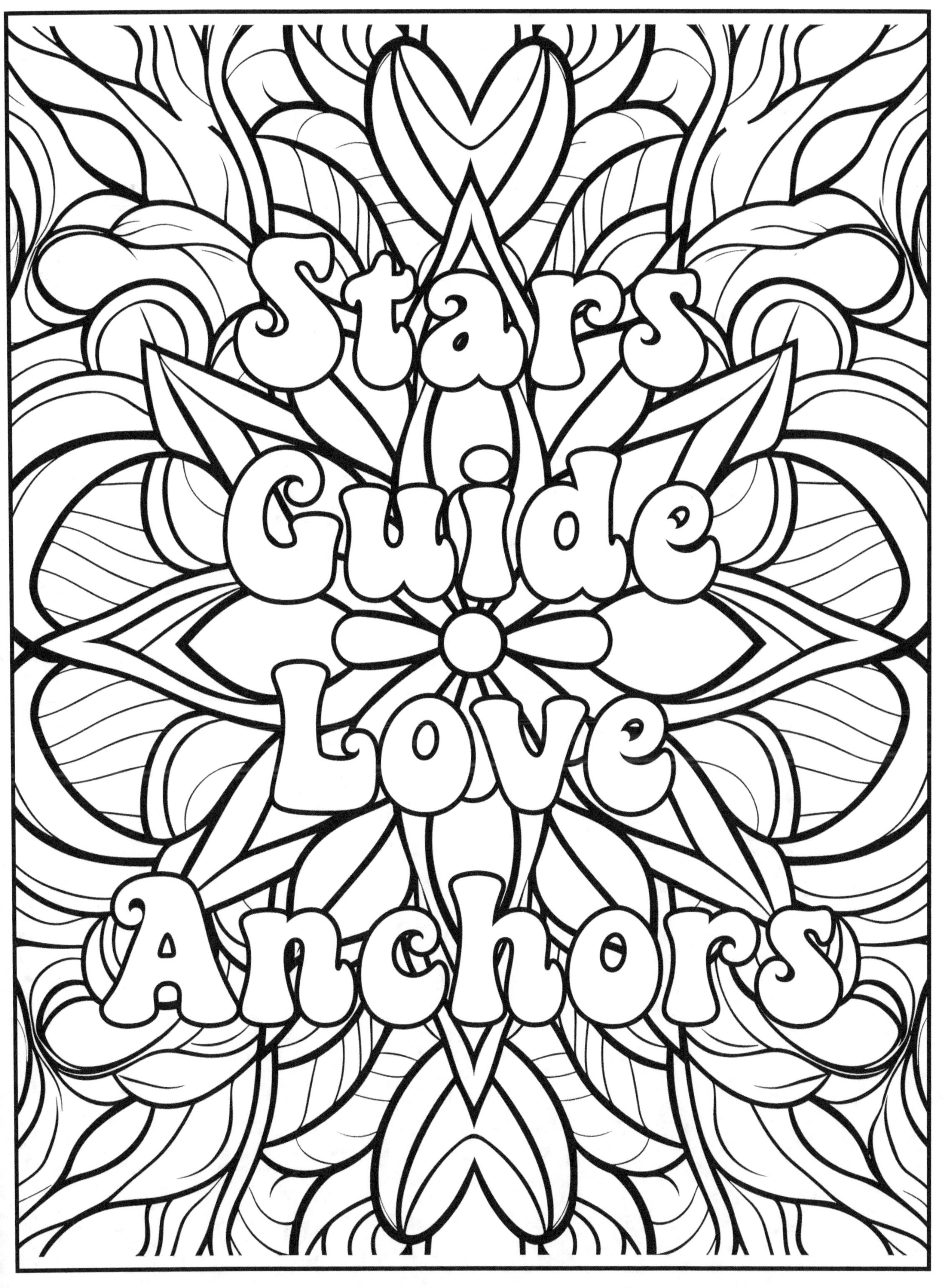

Stars
Guide
Love
Anchors

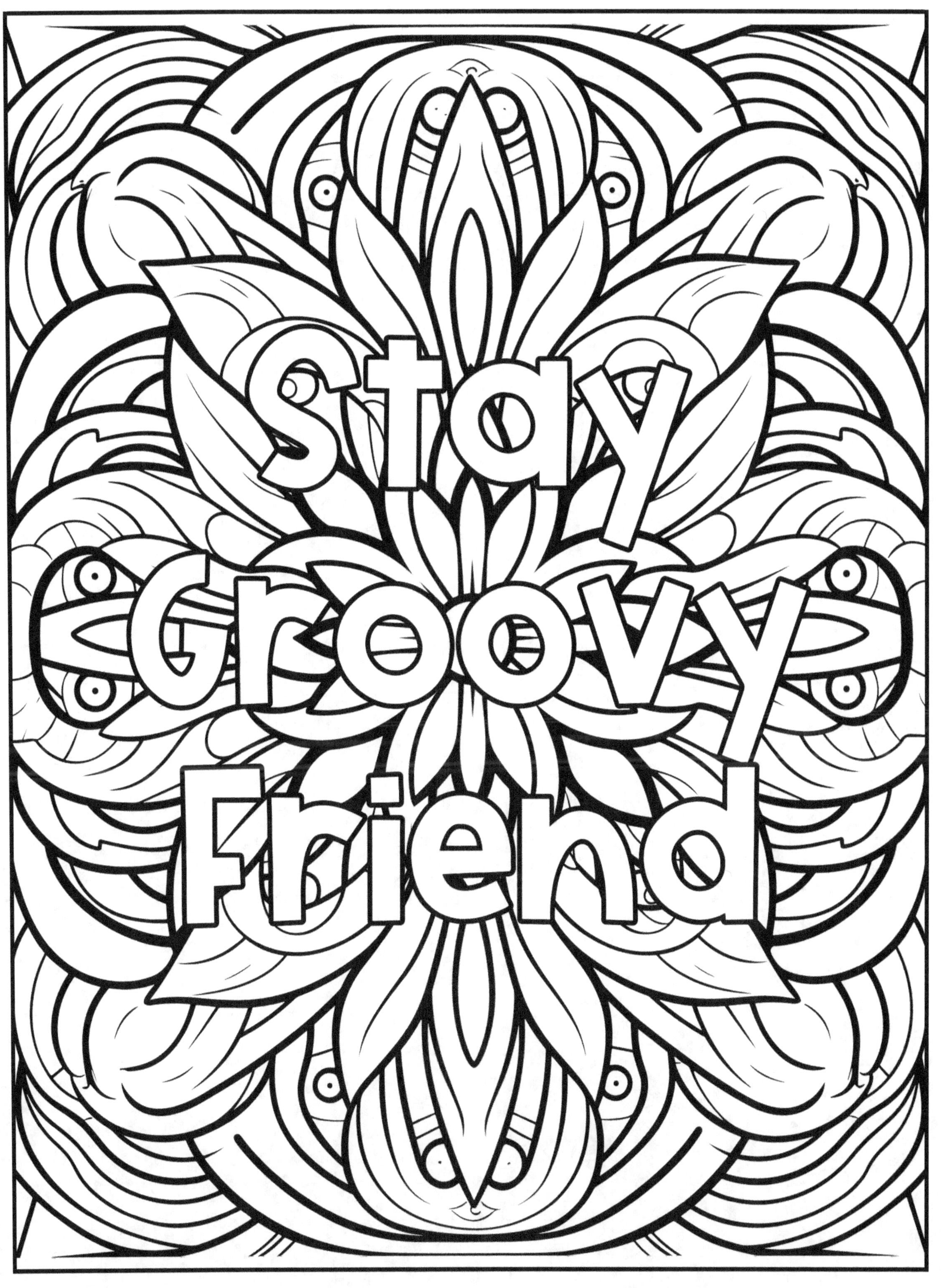

Stay
Groovy
Friend

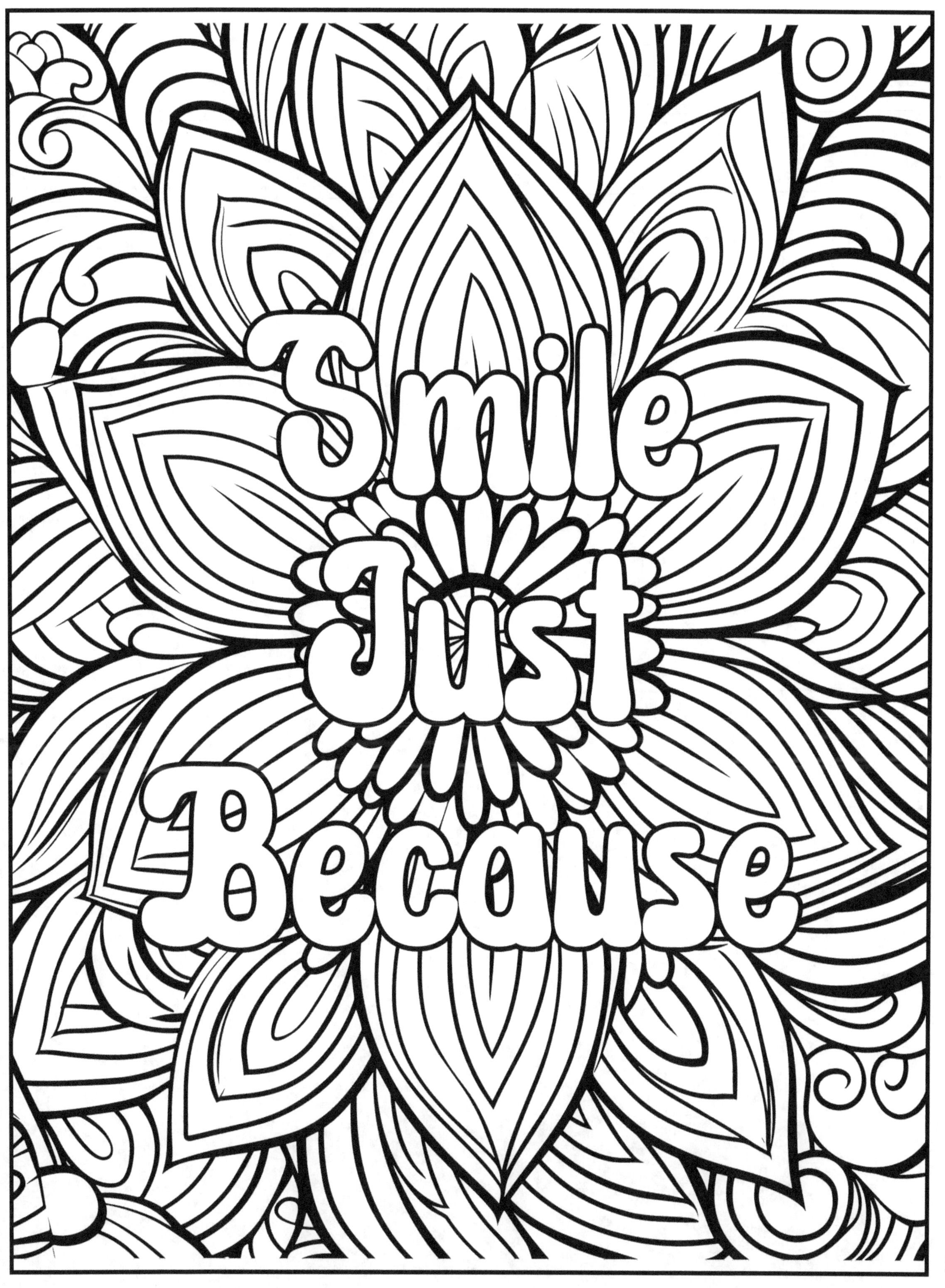

Smile
Just
Because

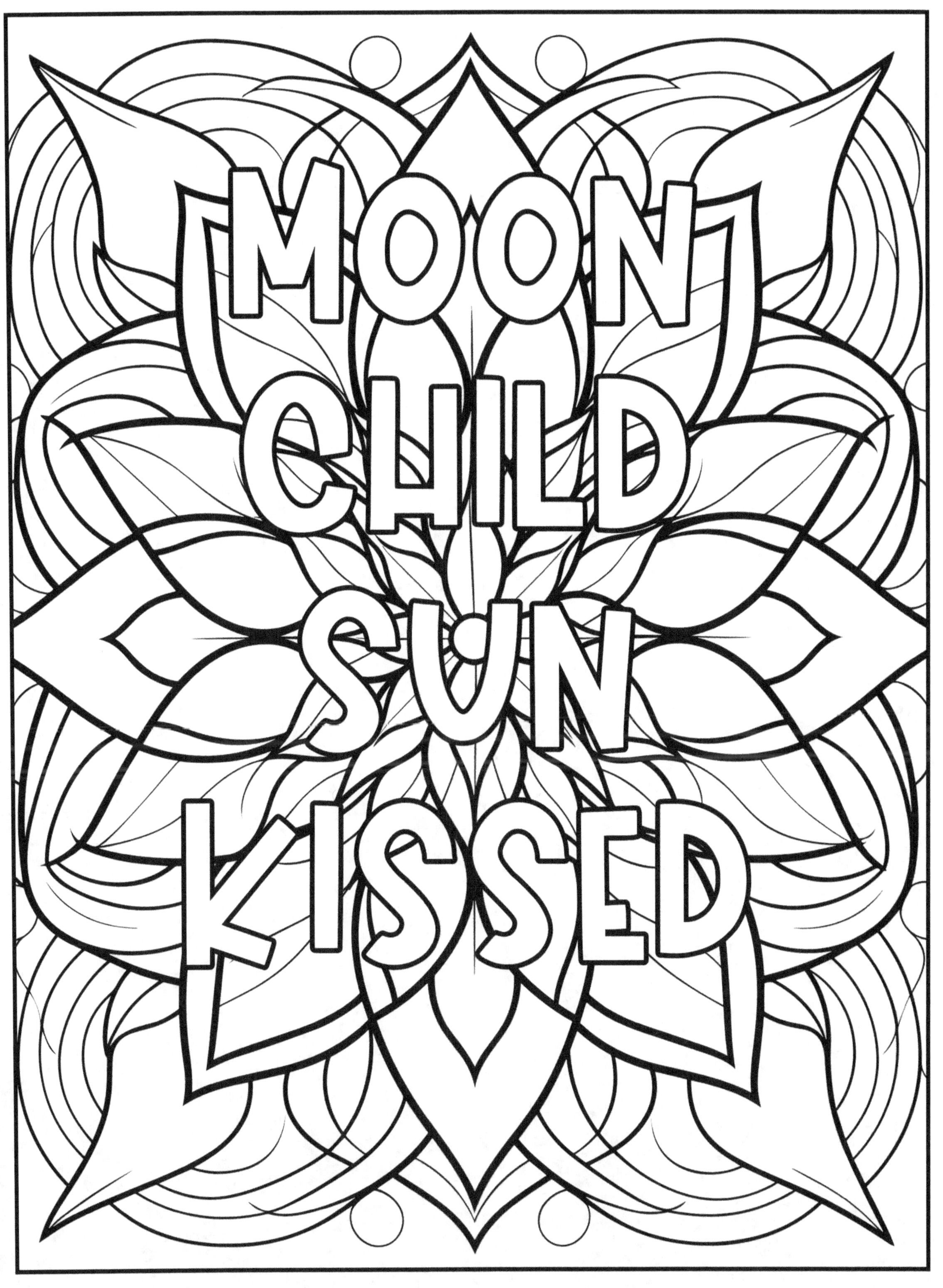

MOON
CHILD
SUN
KISSED

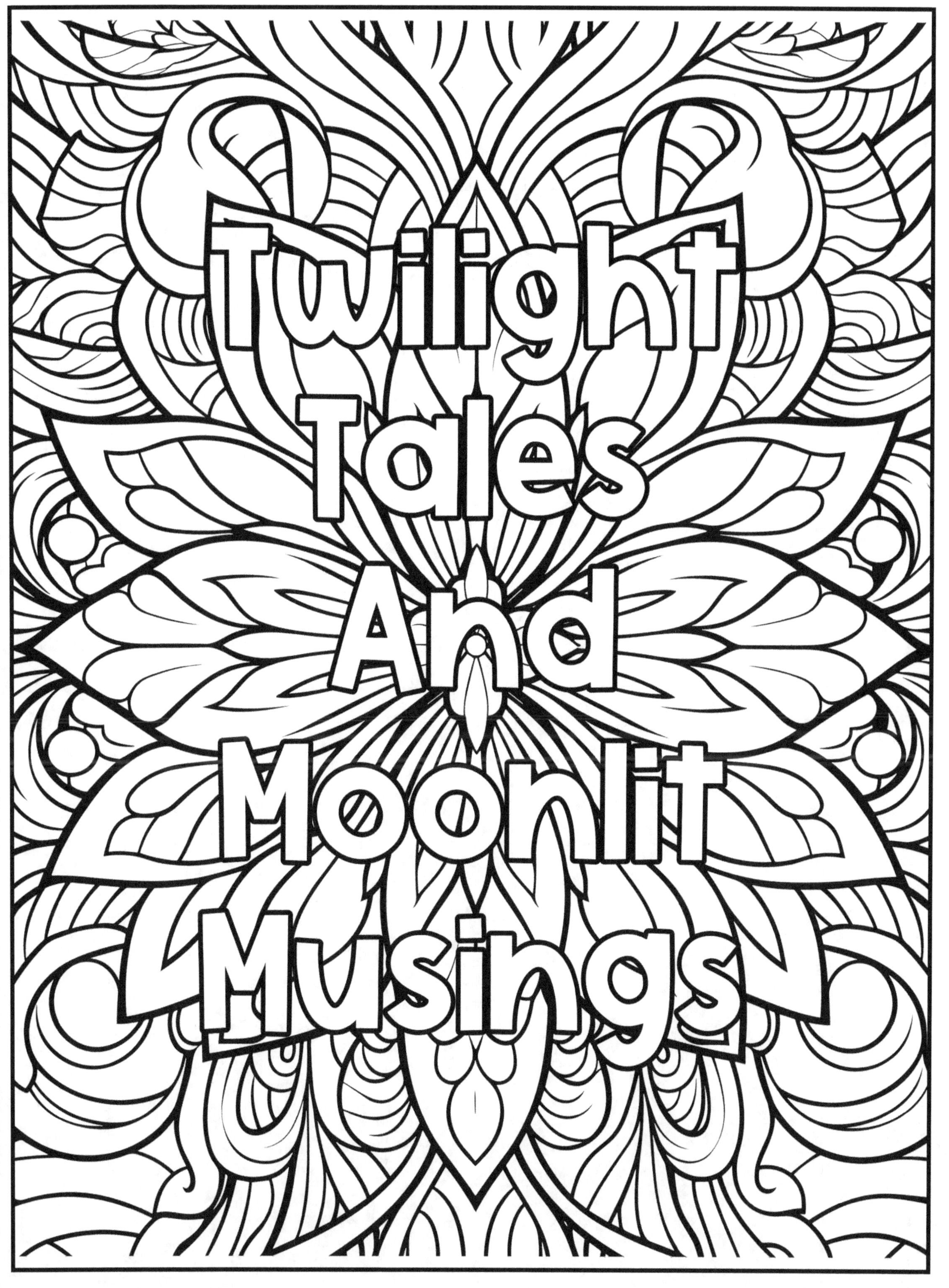

Twilight
Tales
And
Moonlit
Musings

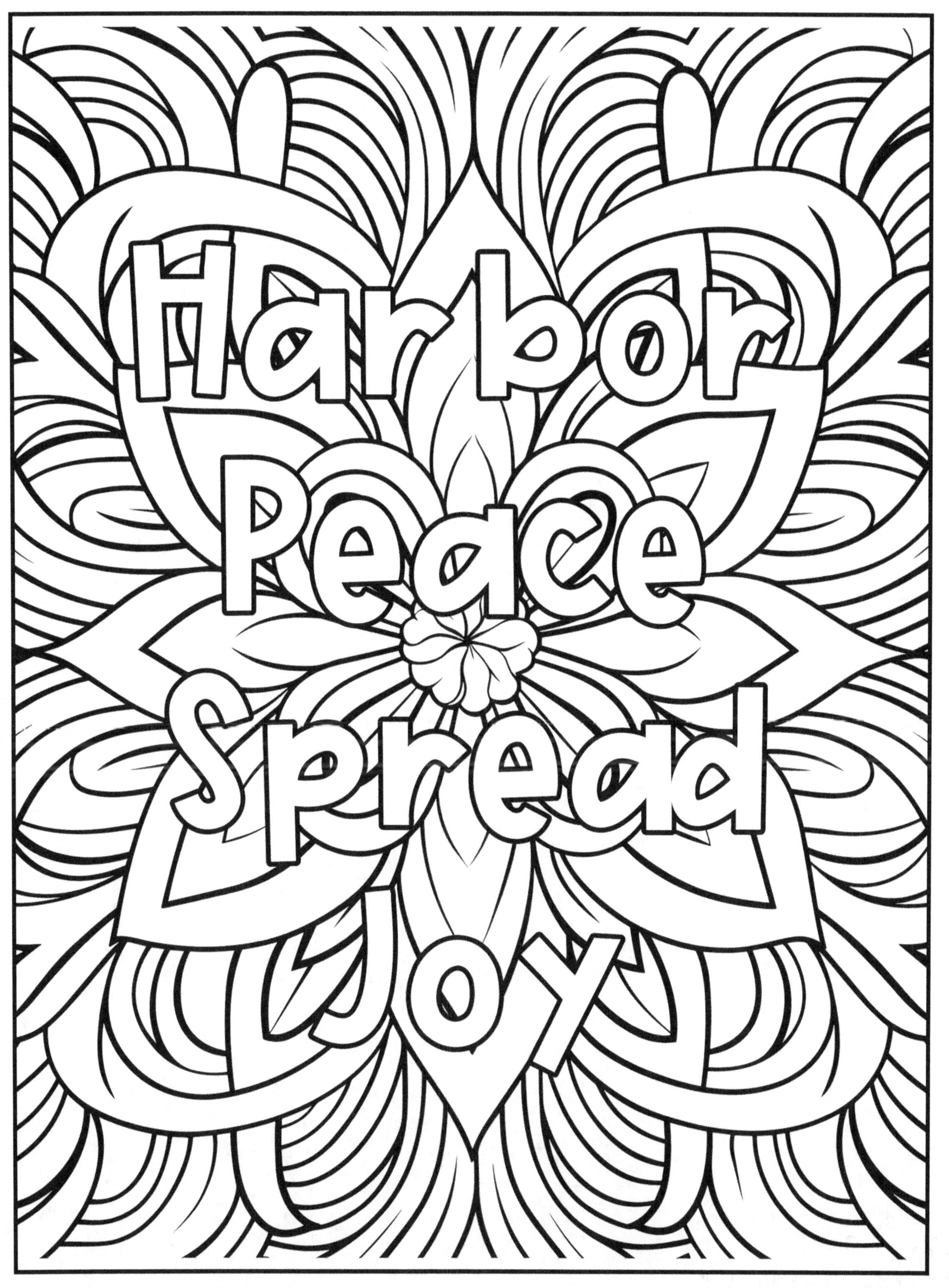

Harbor
Peace
Spread
Joy